Bible Stories
for Grown-Ups

Bible Stories for Grown-Ups
Reading Scripture with New Eyes

Bible Stories for Grown-Ups
978-1-7910-2662-2
978-1-7910-2663-9 eBook

Bible Stories for Grown-Ups: DVD
978-1-7910-2666-0

Bible Stories for Grown-Ups: Leader Guide
978-1-7910-2664-6
978-1-7910-2665-3 eBook

Josh Scott

Bible Stories for Grown-Ups

READING SCRIPTURE WITH NEW EYES

Abingdon Press | Nashville

Bible Stories for Grown-Ups
Reading Scripture with New Eyes

Library of Congress Control Number: 2022949859
978-1-7910-2662-2

MANUFACTURED IN THE UNITED STATES OF AMERICA

*In memory of Dennis Kinkade,
who embodied the curiosity,
openness, and wonder that the
Christian tradition desperately needs.*

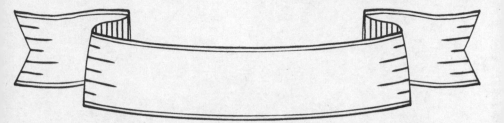

Contents

Introduction ix

Preventing the Flood: The Story of Noah 1

A New Vision of God: The Binding of Isaac 19

It's Not About the Fish: The Story of Jonah 37

Jesus in Unexpected Places: The Parable of the Talents 55

When Repentance Isn't Enough: Looking for Zacchaeus 75

Updating Our Lenses: Healing the Man Who Was Blind 95

Postscript: Where Do We Go from Here? 115

Notes 121

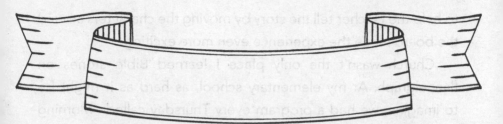

Introduction

THE FLANNELGRAPH EXPERIENCE

This is a book about Bible stories. I'm sure that was pretty clear from the cover. So, let me just begin by placing my cards on the table, so you know exactly what you're getting into in the pages that follow. Here goes: I love the Bible. Whew! Feels good to get that out in the open right off the bat. I do, I love the Bible. It's a passion for me that stretches back to my earliest memories.

My love for the Bible began in a little, white, cinder block church, that was located up a holler in eastern Kentucky. Each Sunday the kids would go down the narrow staircase to the basement where our Sunday school classes would meet for the hour before church started. It was in those classrooms that I experienced the most cutting-edge Sunday school technology of the 1980s: flannelgraph. If this is unfamiliar to you, let me describe it for you. Imagine a board covered in a flannel/felt-like material, resting on an easel. Then cutouts of Bible characters are placed on the surface of the board that create an image of the story that's being taught. In a world of smart devices that allow the streaming of music and video at our fingertips, this might seem like a limited and primitive approach to storytelling, but in those childhood days, the use of flannelgraph brought the stories of the Bible to life in brand-new ways. Of course, those times when I was chosen to help the teacher tell the story by moving the characters around the board made the experience even more exciting.

Church wasn't the only place I learned Bible stories on flannelgraph. At my elementary school, as hard as it might be to imagine, we had a program every Thursday called "Morning Stars." Each week we would go to the auditorium, take a seat, and experience a Bible story brought to life on flannelgraph, complete with a song that helped us memorize the events that had unfolded before our eyes. As a kid, I could not remember the name of the woman who led the program, so I called her Mrs. Morning Star. While it seems strange now to have such an assembly at a public school, I remember those moments fondly. She was a kind person, and, to this day, I still find myself humming some of the songs she taught us during those weekly meetings. Both of those experiences, Sunday school and Morning Stars, instilled in me a curiosity and appreciation for the Bible that are still with me today.

AN IMPOSED LENS

What I was unaware of at the time is that I wasn't just being taught stories. That's not really possible, is it? Throughout my life I have heard pastors say, and probably said myself, some form of: "I'm not telling you my opinion; I'm just telling you what the Bible says." Is that a familiar phrase for you? Here's the problem with it: It just isn't true. Even if we assume the very best about someone saying this, meaning it's not a manipulation or power grab, but comes from an honest place of believing that they are doing, in fact, what they claim, it's not possible. Because the moment we begin talking about what a passage of the Bible means, we are now firmly in the realm of interpretation.

When I was in elementary school, we used to try to be sneaky and look in the back of the teacher's edition of our textbook, because all of the answers were back there. It was simple, the questions had objective answers and they could be known, for sure, and they were all there in the last pages of that teacher's edition book. The Bible doesn't work that way. When we interpret the Bible, we are not coming from a place of objectivity. Instead, we are looking through the lenses we have inherited or developed, like a pair of eyeglasses or contacts. Those lenses are made of up our experiences, how we were taught to see or interpret a particular passage, and all that we collect, consciously and subconsciously, over time.

When we interpret the Bible, we are not coming from a place of objectivity. Instead, we are looking through the lenses we have inherited or developed.

In those early days of childhood, a lens was imposed onto me. To be clear, I am not saying this was a sinister or calculated plan. It can't be helped, actually. When I was being taught a particular story, and discussion happened about the meaning of that particular story, there was no other option but for someone to tell me what she or he understood the story to mean. That person's understanding is what I'm calling a lens. It was likely made up of layers and layers of experiences and classes and sermons that, over time, served to create an interpretation.

The important thing to acknowledge is that we all bring lenses with us, even if we are largely unaware of them, and those lenses impact how we interpret the Bible. Further, our lenses can be refined and even replaced as our understanding grows and changes over time. Actually, I think that is a sign of health, that we update our lenses as we learn and grow.

CHILDHOOD AND GROWN-UP LENSES

In this study, my hope is to help us practically engage what I am calling a "grown-up lens." This grown-up lens stands in contrast to the childhood lens most of us inherited in our earliest experiences of the Bible. Neither of these is meant negatively. I don't call the earliest lens "childish," which carries the idea that it's silly or immature. I mean just the opposite, actually. Childhood is where we all begin, learning and engaging the world through the lenses we are given, that are age-appropriate and extremely helpful in that stage. We shouldn't expect children to engage Bible stories in the same way an adult would. I learned this lesson the hard way with my oldest child. One day, around the age of three or four, he was in the bath, playing with toys in a sea of bubbles, and he asked me about the story of Jonah. That story has always fascinated me, and part of what I have learned over time is that the point of the story isn't whether or not a guy was swallowed by a fish (we'll unpack this story in a later chapter). The story is actually more about what God is like, and as a result how Jonah will respond to his enemies in light of that information, than it is about a guy spending three days and nights in the belly of a fish. I really wanted my son to know this. After giving him way too much information he looked at me and said, "Never mind." Lesson learned. It's important to engage people in age-appropriate ways, which reminds me of Paul's words in 1 Corinthians 13:

When I was a child, I spoke like a child, I thought like a child, I reasoned like a child. When I became an adult, I put an end to childish ways.

(1 Corinthians 13:11)

He doesn't look condescendingly down upon his childhood expressions. He doesn't seem embarrassed that he once communicated and thought like a child. He owns it (the translation above is making an interpretive decision to portray what Paul is talking about as "childish," because the word used is actually just the word for "minor" or "child"), he isn't in opposition to it. But he's also not there anymore. He's grown, he's learned, he can't see things the same way anymore, and that isn't a betrayal or an unfaithfulness. It's how it's all meant to work. One isn't better than the other, both the childhood and grown-up lenses have their places in our development.

WHAT IS A GROWN-UP LENS?

What does a grown-up lens mean, practically? How does it shape how we read and interpret the Bible? As we think about these questions, I want to acknowledge that this description of a grown-up lens is based on my own learning and experiences. Others might differ in places, make additions or subtractions to match their understanding. In what follows I'll offer a sketch, by no means the absolute or be-all and end-all, of what I mean by a "grown-up lens."

First, a grown-up lens makes space for curiosity. In my experience, curiosity is at the core of the journey of transformation. I'm reminded of the story of Moses's calling in Exodus chapter 3. While taking care of his father-in-law's flocks, Moses sees a bush that, while on fire, was not consumed by the flames. Moses's response was to pay attention to the curiosity the sight of the burning bush had sparked.

> *Then Moses said, "I must turn aside and look at this great sight*
> *and see why the bush is not burned up.*
>
> (Exodus 3:3)

In the narrative of the Exodus, it was this moment, Moses paying attention to his curiosity, that launched the pivotal story that underlies the entirety of the biblical narrative. Imagine if Moses had chosen, in fear, to douse the burning bush instead of to investigate? Fear is the enemy of curiosity, and as a result, one of the greatest limiters of our transformation.

As we move through these six stories, I encourage you to read each one through before beginning the chapter. While reading, pay attention to what stands out for you. Does anything seem strange? Out of place? Is there anything that raises questions or makes a connection? I know for so many of us, the idea of bringing a real sense of curiosity to the Bible, including the doubts and questions we carry, is scary. The good news is, it's not out of line with our spiritual ancestors. They engaged in creative and curious readings of the Bible, and that allowed them to make connections and discoveries over time that radically transformed, not only them, but the Christian tradition itself.

Second, a grown-up lens takes the Bible seriously, and it's important that we understand what that means. One of the ways I used to read the Bible was to try to decide which parts of it were literally, meaning historically, true and which parts were perhaps parable or metaphorical. Many of the stories we will explore in this book were some of the same ones I used to agonize over. Was there a great flood, like the one in Genesis 6? Did Jonah really end up being swallowed by a fish? How literally should we take the stories of the miraculous in the Bible? Those questions were at the center of my engagement with the Bible for years, and my frustrations grew and grew as a result. Here's the good news: that question is not a focus of this book. I have realized over the years that the "did-it-or-didn't-it" question is ultimately unanswerable. Regardless of our perspective, there does not exist a source of objective proof (like the teacher's edition of a textbook), which means we spend an inordinate amount of time trying to discover the undiscoverable.

The approach I am taking to these stories is not dependent on whether they did or didn't happen literally. The question we will ask as the center of our discussion is "What do these stories mean?" Here's why this shift in focus matters, even though I'm sure it seems simple and obvious: When we focus on meaning, on what the writers are trying to communicate, we are actually engaging their work in ways that can be productive. Even if we could somehow definitively prove that Jonah was swallowed and survived three days in the belly of a fish, what does that matter (besides the shock factor of it) if we don't attempt to discern what the story means? That approach, meaning, will be the aim of this study.

Further, understanding the context of a story matters critically. When I was in college, I was part of a summer ministry team that ran a youth camp. Each morning our staff would get together and, before we ate breakfast, someone would open the oversized family-style Bible in the lobby and, with closed eyes, point to a passage. That was the "verse of the day," and sometimes we ended up with some hilarious or awkward passages. While we were just having fun, this is sometimes a way we approach the Bible. We take a random verse from here and another from there and create a patchwork, cherry-picked theology that, sometimes, can even work against the possible meanings of the texts.

In the interpretations that I will offer in the pages ahead, my goal is to situate each story within the larger contexts in which they are grounded. For example, we will ask questions about what was happening in the world around the authors when each story was likely written. The writers of what we now call Scripture didn't write in a vacuum. Their stories were born out of and were responses to the events transpiring around them. To be able to offer plausible interpretations of these stories, then, it is helpful to know the exterior pressures and events that shaped the communities and authors that produced the literature that came to be part of the Bible. It's also fascinating when we get a glimpse of how a particular author, say whoever wrote the story of Noah and the Great Flood, is interacting with the interpretations of other cultures around him or her.

Another important context is how the stories function within the larger canon of Scripture. This will become evident as we go, but perhaps we'll see it most in the last chapter, which will seek to locate the meaning of a strange healing story from the Gospel of Mark. That story is tied to something much larger that Mark is doing, and when we can allow ourselves to step back and see it, it's absolutely brilliant. I think of it as reaching cruising altitude on an airplane and then looking back down at the ground and seeing how all these parcels of land connect beneath you.

**We aren't just interested in the past,
but in what the past might say
to our present and future.**

Like any library, the Bible contains various kinds of literature, and sometimes the different books interact and converse with what came before. This is true throughout both the Hebrew Bible and the New Testament. Stories build in layers, with later authors interacting with older texts, and in doing so creating new meanings and interpretations to meet the moments in which they lived. That's an important part of why we engage with the Bible, isn't it? We aren't just interested in the past, but in what the past might say to our present and future.

Which means another important feature of a grown-up lens is to responsibly apply the meanings we locate in the Bible to the contexts in which we find ourselves today. That means we immerse ourselves into the context of the Bible and then creatively listen for how the meaning of a story or passage speaks to our world. At the end of each chapter, I'll take some time to ask the "what now" or "what does it mean for us" question and then offer some suggestions for how we might make those connections from the past to the present. My suggestions are just that and by no means exhaustive. My hope is that you will find yourself, as you move through the stories and interpretations, creatively reimagining what these stories might have to say to us in the world in which we find ourselves.

Before we begin, let's take just a moment for an overview of where we are going in the chapters that follow. I have selected the six Bible stories we will explore because they are well-known, offer what I think is a powerful message for our current moment, and they all also offer some surprises along the way.

WHERE WE ARE GOING

Each chapter of this book will take us into a well-known story from the Bible. Many of these stories will feel so familiar that you might wonder how in the world any other interpretations might even be possible. Let me encourage you to not rush to judgment or assume anything about these stories. Try to open yourself up to the surprises we might uncover when we seek to situate and engage these old, old stories through a grown-up lens that prioritizes the contexts in which they were written. I'll also challenge you to remain open to the ways these ancient stories can still speak to our context in surprising and challenging ways. The Bible might be a library of stories, poems, and letters from more than two millennia ago, but it also continues to resonate and offer insight into how we might engage the world in transformative and beautiful ways today.

In chapter 1, we'll explore the story of Noah and the Flood. I'd argue this story is perhaps the most widely known narrative from the Bible in our culture, saturating our imagination. For many people, the story of Noah has dramatically shaped their notion of God and God's character. It's also interesting that this story is commonly represented on the cover of children's Bibles and found adorning nurseries in homes and children's space in churches. What about this story seems kid-friendly? What might a grown-up lens teach us about the deeper meanings of Noah's story for us today? That's coming in Chapter One.

As we turn to chapter 2, we'll stay in the early pages of the Bible with the story of Abraham's near sacrifice of Isaac. This is a story that has troubled many readers over the years. Like Noah, this story has given so much shape to how readers envision God, and how God interacts with humans. Some questions we will focus on as we explore this story are about just that: Is that what God is like? Does God demand from us? How does this story speak to us in this particular moment? I think you'll be surprised at the timeliness of this story for our own moment.

In chapter 3, we will look at one final story from the Hebrew Bible, and it's one that rivals the Noah story in our cultural imagination. I'm talking, of course, about the story of Jonah. There's something about this story that is both gripping and concerning. On the one hand, even if it were not a story from the Bible, it would make a fantastic tale or movie. Can you imagine the special effects opportunities? But is this story primarily about the bad things that could happen to us if we run from God's commands, or is there something even more challenging, especially in this moment in history?

Beginning in chapter 4, we will turn to the New Testament. Jesus regularly communicated his understanding of the kingdom of God through the use of parables. These stories about farmers, soils, and lost things give us a window into what Jesus envisioned for the world, and how that vision would be realized. The parable we will examine is often called "The Parable of the Talents." Most often it's interpreted as being about what we do with the gifts, abilities, and responsibilities with which God entrusts us. Will we engage them for God, or will we bury them in selfishness? However, I have found that, within context, this story is doing something else, something surprising, that might help us understand more deeply what Jesus thought he was up to in his Kingdom work.

Chapter 5 focuses on a story that, for many of us, has been preserved in our consciousness because of the song we learned as children. What does the encounter between Jesus and Zacchaeus teach us about the mission of Jesus? Further, what does Zacchaeus's response to Jesus say about what it means to take following Jesus seriously? As we examine this story, I think there will be more than a couple surprises as we get to know Zacchaeus and the impact he made on his community.

In chapter 6, we will discuss the story of a healing Jesus performed, restoring the sight of a man who was blind. This isn't your run-of-the-mill healing story, however. This story sees Jesus's first attempt at restoring the man's sight met with only a partial healing. It took a second attempt to fully return the man's vision.

While this is an unexpected turn of events—after all Jesus in other places in the Gospels heals with just a word, from a distance—if we understand what might be happening here, it can help us appreciate the challenge of being Jesus's disciple, both then and now.

Finally, in the Postscript, I'll draw together a few thoughts about all that we've learned, and where we might go from here as we continue to engage the stories of the Bible (if you choose to do so). The stories might be someone else's mail, but we have found them entrusted to our care. That means how we engage them—how we interpret them—matters.

The Bible looms large over our culture. It's been the impetus for both much good and much terror. As a pastor I regularly meet people who struggle with the Bible. They've experienced the pain of having the Bible used against them as a club. It's been weaponized against them, causing deep pain. They are unsure about how, if at all, they can interact with it. If that's you, let's just imagine for a moment we are meeting at a coffee shop to chat. You might feel a little nervous about having the conversation. Maybe you even feel a sense of grief, because, while at one point the Bible was a meaningful part of your life, now you don't know if you and the Bible have a future together. Let's take a deep breath. It's okay. Those questions you have are valid. The things you've noticed in some of the stories that don't add up, or that you've never gotten a good response about, they don't make you an enemy of the Bible. They actually mean you care enough to read it closely and take it seriously. That's what we will do in the pages that follow. We will take the Bible seriously. We'll put on our grown-up lenses and make space for our questions and curiosities. Perhaps, in the process, we'll be surprised at what we find and don't find.

My great hope is that if you are one of the growing number of people who have lost the Bible—or more accurately, had it stolen from you through misuse and trauma—and you feel grief around that, I hope in these pages I can begin to offer a path for you to reengage in ways that are healing. I hope we can adopt a new set of lenses that bring into focus the subversive, radical nature of many of these stories. I hope we can begin to reimagine a way of engaging the Bible that isn't about proof-texting or proving our rightness and their wrongness but is instead an invitation to participate in the ever-unfolding work of bringing heaven to earth. It will require a willingness to see differently, to trade in our expired lenses for new ones that will give us a more sharp and focused vision. We need grown-up lenses because these stories really weren't written for children. They were written for grown-ups. They are nuanced and complicated, but doing the hard work of reading and interpreting them through these new lenses is worth it, because it opens up to us new layers of understanding and possibility. Perhaps, in embracing these grown-up lenses we might even get a glimpse of the radical, subversive, and transformative nature of these stories—the very things we have missed as a result of the expired lenses of childhood that we've inherited.

Are you up for the journey?

Then, let's begin.

CHAPTER 1

Preventing the Flood: The Story of Noah

Genesis 6-8

FLOOD STORIES

On April 5, 1977, the world stopped in my hometown of Williamson, West Virginia. After days of heavy rain, the "Mighty Tug" Fork River overflowed the flood walls, leaving the city engulfed in thirty to more than fifty feet of water. The breach came so fast that no one had time to prepare or gather belongings. It came without warning, and many people lost everything. My dad was eighteen years old during the '77 flood, and his family was counted among those who could salvage nothing. I was born four years after the devastation, and yet stories about the '77 flood were a regular part of the conversation during my formative years.

It seems that the idea of catastrophic flooding was a fairly common concern and focus in the ancient world, and not just in the Bible. The cultures surrounding, and no doubt influencing, ancient Israel had their own stories of deluge to tell. One now-well-known example comes from the *Epic of Gilgamesh*, an ancient Mesopotamian text that recounts the adventures of an ancient king, you guessed it, Gilgamesh, as he traveled the world searching for immortality. How ancient is this story? Scholars date at least parts of the epic to the twenty-first century BCE, meaning it could very well be the oldest written literature in the world.

The story of the flood, according to *Gilgamesh*, is found on tablet XI, and involves a hero named Utnapishtim. In this story the gods are angry with humans because they are too noisy. The "unceasing clamor" was too much, so the gods devise a plan to destroy human life through a great deluge. They all agreed to keep the plan a secret, but Ea, the god of wisdom, found a loophole. He went to the home of Utnapishtim, which was made of reeds, and spoke the secret to the reeds. Utnapishtim heard the news, of course, and followed Ea's wisdom. He tore down his home and repurposed the materials to build a boat on which he and his family, and "the seed of every creature that lives upon the earth," could escape the coming flood. The waters rose so high that even the gods became frightened by what they had unleashed on the earth. The storm lasted six days, and on the seventh the waters receded, and eventually the boat came to rest on a mountain. Utnapishtim released a dove, then a swallow, but both returned because they couldn't find a resting place. Finally, he released a raven, which did not return, giving the indication that it was safe to leave the confines of the boat. Utnapishtim offered a sacrifice to the gods, who happen to show up and grant both him and his wife immortality. This story ends with a rainbow in the sky, and pledge to never again send the flood waters to destroy the earth.

It's a fascinating story, isn't it? I also find it a really import-ant backdrop for a "grown-up" reading of the story of the Great

Flood found in the Book of Genesis. The Bible wasn't written in a vacuum; it was written in a context that contained many voices telling many stories that were trying to make sense of the world and their place in it. So, try to keep the story I've just shared in mind as we move into the biblical story of Noah.

As we begin thinking about the story of Noah and the Great Flood, it's important for us to start with an overview that will orient us to the details of the narrative as they are found in the Bible. Below are two different versions of the Noah and the Great Flood story. Take a moment to read through both of these examples, paying attention to how they are similar, and how they are different. Which one of these stories is found in the Book of Genesis (no peeking!)?

Example A

The LORD saw that the wickedness of humankind was great in the earth, and that every inclination of the thoughts of their hearts was only evil continually. And the LORD was sorry that he had made humankind on the earth, and it grieved him to his heart. So the LORD said, "I will blot out from the earth the human beings I have created—people together with animals and creeping things and birds of the air, for I am sorry that I have made them." But Noah found favor in the sight of the LORD.

Then the LORD said to Noah, "Go into the ark, you and all your household, for I have seen that you alone are righteous before me in this generation. Take with you seven pairs of all clean animals, the male and its mate; and a pair of the animals that are not clean, the male and its mate; and seven pairs of the birds of the air also, male and female, to keep their kind alive on the face of all the earth. For in seven days I will send rain on the earth for forty days and forty nights; and every living thing that I have made I will blot out from the face of the ground." And Noah did all that the LORD had commanded him. And Noah with his sons and his wife and his sons' wives went into the ark to escape the waters of the flood. And after seven days the waters of the flood came on the earth. The rain fell on the earth forty days and forty nights, and the LORD shut him in.

The flood continued forty days on the earth; and the waters increased, and bore up the ark, and it rose high above the earth. The waters swelled and increased greatly on the earth; and the ark floated on the face of the waters. The waters swelled so mightily on the earth that all the high mountains under the whole heaven were covered; the waters swelled above the mountains, covering them fifteen cubits deep. Everything on dry land in whose nostrils was the breath of life died. He blotted out every living thing that was on the face of the ground, human beings and animals and creeping things and birds of the air; they were blotted out from the earth. Only Noah was left, and those that were with him in the ark

At the end of forty days Noah opened the window of the ark that he had made. Then he sent out the dove from him, to see if the waters had subsided from the face of the ground; but the dove found no place to set its foot, and it returned to him to the ark, for the waters were still on the face of the whole earth. So he put out his hand and took it and brought it into the ark with him. He waited another seven days, and again he sent out the dove from the ark; and the dove came back to him in the evening, and there in its beak was a freshly plucked olive leaf; so Noah knew that the waters had subsided from the earth. Then he waited another seven days, and sent out the dove; and it did not return to him anymore. And Noah removed the covering of the ark, and looked, and saw that the face of the ground was drying. Then Noah built an altar to the LORD, and took of every clean animal and of every clean bird, and offered burnt offerings on the altar. As long as the earth endures, seedtime and harvest, cold and heat, summer and winter, day and night, shall not cease.

And when the LORD smelled the pleasing odor, the LORD said in his heart, "I will never again curse the ground because of humankind, for the inclination of the human heart is evil from youth; nor will I ever again destroy every living creature as I have done."

Example B

These are the descendants of Noah. Noah was a righteous man, blameless in his generation; Noah walked with God. And Noah had three sons, Shem, Ham, and Japheth.

Now the earth was corrupt in God's sight, and the earth was filled with violence. And God saw that the earth was corrupt; for all flesh had corrupted its ways upon the earth. And God said to Noah, "I have determined to make an end of all flesh, for the earth is filled with violence because of them; now I am going to destroy them along with the earth. Make yourself an ark of cypress wood; make rooms in the ark, and cover it inside and out with pitch. This is how you are to make it: the length of the ark three hundred cubits, its width fifty cubits, and its height thirty cubits. Make a roof for the ark, and finish it to a cubit above; and put the door of the ark in its side; make it with lower, second, and third decks. For my part, I am going to bring a flood of waters on the earth, to destroy from under heaven all flesh in which is the breath of life; everything that is on the earth shall die. But I will establish my covenant with you; and you shall come into the ark, you, your sons, your wife, and your sons' wives with you. And of every living thing, of all flesh, you shall bring two of every kind into the ark, to keep them alive with you; they shall be male and female. Of the birds according to their kinds, and of the animals according to their kinds, of every creeping thing of the ground according to its kind, two of every kind shall come in to you, to keep them alive. Also take with you every kind of food that is eaten, and store it up; and it shall serve as food for you and for them." Noah did this; he did all that God commanded him.

Noah was six hundred years old when the flood of waters came on the earth. Of clean animals, and of animals that are not clean, and of birds, and of everything that creeps on the ground, two and two, male and female, went into the ark with Noah, as God had commanded Noah.

In the six hundredth year of Noah's life, in the second month, on the seventeenth day of the month, on that day all the fountains of the great deep burst forth, and the windows of the heavens were opened. On the very same day Noah with his sons, Shem and Ham and Japheth, and Noah's wife and the three wives of his sons entered the ark, they and every wild animal of every kind, and all domestic animals of every kind, and every creeping thing that creeps on the earth, and every bird of every kind— every bird, every winged creature. They went into the ark with Noah, two and two of all flesh in which there was the breath of life. And those that entered, male and female of all flesh, went in as God had commanded him; and all flesh died that moved on the earth, birds, domestic animals, wild animals, all swarming creatures that swarm on the earth, and all human beings; and the waters swelled on the earth for one hundred fifty days.

But God remembered Noah and all the wild animals and all the domestic animals that were with him in the ark. And God made a wind blow over the earth, and the waters subsided; the fountains of the deep and the windows of the heavens were closed, the rain from the heavens was restrained, and the waters gradually receded from the earth. At the end of one hundred fifty days the waters had abated; and in the seventh month, on the seventeenth day of the month, the ark came to rest on the mountains of Ararat. The waters continued to abate until the tenth month; in the tenth month, on the first day of the month, the tops of the mountains appeared. And he sent out the raven; and it went to and fro until the waters were dried up from the earth.

In the six hundred first year, in the first month, on the first day of the month, the waters were dried up from the earth; in the second month, on the twenty-seventh day of the month, the earth was dry. Then God said to Noah, "Go out of the ark, you and your wife, and your sons and your sons' wives with you. Bring out with you every living thing that is with you of all flesh— birds and animals and every creeping thing that creeps on the earth—so that they may abound on the earth, and be fruitful and multiply on the earth." So Noah went out with his sons and his wife and his sons' wives. And every animal, every creeping thing, and every bird, everything that moves on the earth, went out of the ark by families.

Having read both of these examples, what do you notice? There are similarities to be sure, but also really interesting differences. By what name is God called in each story? How many pairs of animals board the ark? How long does the flood last? What kind of bird is sent out? It might help to use different colored highlighters to mark the differences visually.

Scholars have a general agreement that the first five books of the Bible are made up of at least four different sources.

The big question is, which example is the one found in the Bible? It turns out to be a bit of a trick question, because the answer is both! Scholars have a general agreement that the first five books of the Bible, often called *Torah* (meaning "Instruction") or *Pentateuch* (meaning "five books"), are made up of at least four different sources. Those sources reflect different locations and times in which the stories that make up the Torah were

7

written. For example, it's why some places and people have different names in different places. Did Moses encounter God on Mt. Sinai or Horeb? Both, depending on the source. Was Moses's father-in-law named Jethro or Reuel or Hobab? Depends on the source. That is also true for the story, or should I say stories, of Noah and the Great Flood.

The first reading (Example A) comes from a source called the *Yahwist* due to the use of the personal divine name for God, *Yahweh* (and represented by *J*, because the scholars who discovered this were German), the composition of which dates to somewhere between the late tenth to eighth century BCE. Example B is represented by the letter *P*, because it is a source that reflects the concerns of the priestly class. Scholars date this source no later than the sixth or fifth century BCE. I share this to say that both of the Flood stories in the Book of Genesis were composed many years after Gilgamesh, meaning that the authors were possibly aware of, and perhaps responding to, that earlier narrative.

As we begin to view these stories through a grown-up lens, it helps to start with the question why? Specifically, why does the flood come? In *Gilgamesh*, you may recall, the flood comes as a result of the noisiness of humans. People made too large of a racket, and the gods responded with a flood. The story of Noah in Genesis, however, ties the flood to the violence of human beings.

> The LORD saw that the wickedness of humans was great in the earth and that every inclination of the thoughts of their hearts was only evil continually.
>
> *(Genesis 6:5)*

> Now the earth was corrupt in God's sight, and the earth was filled with violence.
>
> *(Genesis 6:11)*

This is a fascinating detail. It also makes me wonder what has happened in the story that led us to this moment, human beings on the brink of extinction as a direct result of their preoccupation with violence. It seems that, before we can really understand what is happening with the story of Noah and the Great Flood, we might need to rewind a bit, so we can understand the larger narrative that is culminating in the eradication of human life from the earth.

SEEING THE LARGER STORY

The Bible begins with a story about creation. God, in this story, speaks and creation begins to take shape and form. The story begins with watery chaos, and God sets about seeking to bring order and creation out of the wildness. On the second day we are told about the creation of the sky:

> And God said, "Let there be a dome in the midst of the waters, and let it separate the waters from the waters." So God made the dome and separated the waters that were under the dome from the waters that were above the dome. And it was so. God called the dome Sky. And there was evening and there was morning, the second day.
>
> (Genesis 1:6-8)

The job of the sky, in the ancient cosmology reflected in Genesis chapter 1, was to be a protective-dome-like-bubble that held back the primordial waters that would, if unleashed, destroy creation. This is an important detail to remember, because our ancient ancestors had a dramatically different understanding of creation than we do now. Let's not be critical, because they (like us) were arriving at the best conclusions based on the information provided to them. They understood the sky to be a barrier between them and the primordial, watery chaos.

This is an important detail because the story of the Great Flood describes the undoing of this protective layer:

> In the six hundredth year of Noah's life, in the second month, on the seventeenth day of the month, on that day all the fountains of the great deep burst forth, and the windows of the heavens were opened. The rain fell on the earth forty days and forty nights.
>
> (Genesis 7:11-12)

According to the narrator of our story, the cause of this catastrophic collapse of the sky was human violence. From where did this violence emerge, and how, only six chapters into the story, can humanity be facing such a cataclysm?

One of my favorite Bible-nerd questions to ask people is, "When is sin first mentioned in the narrative of the Bible?" There is always, inevitably, a pause. The answer seems so obvious that the question seems to be a trick, and it is. The general assumption is that sin enters the story in Genesis chapter 3, when the first humans eat the forbidden fruit from the Tree of the Knowledge of Good and Evil. That's the moment when their eyes are opened, and they realize that they are naked. It's this realization that sends them scrambling for a fig leaf and a place to hide when they hear the sound of God arriving for their evening stroll. Here's the interesting thing: the word *sin* never occurs in Genesis chapter 3. It's just not in there. If you read the text in Hebrew, the word *sin* does not yet make its entrance into the story of the Bible. It does, however, show up in the very next chapter. The story is likely familiar: it's the account of Cain killing his brother Abel.

In this story (found in Genesis chapter 4), the two brothers offer sacrifices to God, Cain from his crops and Abel from his flock. For some reason, we aren't told why, Abel's sacrifice was acceptable to God, but Cain's was not. This rejection made Cain angry and resentful. The text says, "his countenance fell." Then God comes to Cain with a warning:

> The LORD said to Cain, "Why are you angry, and why has your countenance fallen? If you do well, will you not be accepted? And if you do not do well, sin is lurking at the door; its desire is for you, but you must master it."
>
> *(Genesis 4:6-7)*

A couple of things to notice: First, sin officially enters the story with this warning from God about what Cain's anger and resentment will produce if they aren't tended to. Sin, God warns, is seeking to take hold of Cain. The image of sin being used is that of a snake coiled up, ready to strike, or perhaps the image of a cat that is hunkered down, ready to pounce on an unsuspecting mouse. Sin, in this first mention, is singular, not plural. People often ask questions about what is or isn't a sin, or we talk about sins, plural. But sin enters the story as something that is singular. It's not a sin or sins; it's sin. To understand what sin might mean in this story, notice what happens next.

> Cain said to his brother Abel, "Let us go out to the field." And when they were in the field, Cain rose up against his brother Abel and killed him.
>
> *Genesis 4:8*

That line, "Let us go out to the field," gives away what comes next, doesn't it? Imagine this as a scene in a movie. We totally see it coming. Picture Cain with one arm behind his back, perhaps holding a hoe or a rock, and inviting his brother to take a walk. We'd be shouting at the screen, "Don't do it, Abel! It's a trap!" But our warnings go unheard. Two brothers make the journey to the field, and only one comes back. It seems sin, here, is connected to and rooted in human violence. Sin wants to master Cain, and with the slaying of his brother, sin gets what it wants.

From this moment, human violence only escalates. Cain is sent away, with the understanding that anyone who kills him will suffer a sevenfold vengeance (Genesis 4:15). Finally, sometime later, Cain's great-great-great grandson, Lamech, engages in this kind of retaliatory violence. He sings a song to his wives about his action, the poetry masking the reality that he has killed another human being.

> Lamech said to his wives:
> "Adah and Zillah, hear my voice;
>   you wives of Lamech, listen to what I say:
> I have killed a man for wounding me,
>   a young man for striking me.
> If Cain is avenged sevenfold,
>   truly Lamech seventy-sevenfold."
>   (Genesis 4:23-24)

Notice the escalation of retaliatory violence—if Cain is avenged sevenfold, Lamech is avenged seventy-sevenfold. Human violence is not dissipating with each successive generation but multiplying and creating the context for the story of Noah and the Great Flood: the earth is full of human violence.

How bad has it gotten on the earth six chapters into the story? Human violence has unleashed the primordial, chaotic waters. A creation that had been integrated is becoming dis-integrated. The order spoken into existence by God is being dis-ordered. The result is the collapse and destruction of human life and civilization.

> And all flesh died that moved on the earth, birds, domestic animals, wild animals, all swarming creatures that swarm on the earth, and all human beings; everything on dry land in whose nostrils was the breath of life died.
>   (Genesis 7:21-22)

However, Noah and his family were safe on the ark. After the waters receded, evidenced by the failure of the dove (or raven, depending on the source) to return, they disembarked, made an offering to God, and received from God what is known as the Noahic covenant. This was a promise from God to all humanity that never again would this kind of deluge happen:

> *"I establish my covenant with you, that never again shall all flesh be cut off by the waters of a flood, and never again shall there be a flood to destroy the earth."*
>
> (Genesis 9:11)

IT'S ALL ABOUT MEANING

Maybe you're asking the same question right now that I often ask about stories like this, which would be: "What do we do with it?" Right? It's not enough to just say, "Well, it's in the Bible." We have to wrestle with what it means, because these stories weren't written to relay facts about events. They were written to invite us into meaning.

First, I think it's important to name the fact that stories like Noah and the Great Flood aren't kid friendly. Have you ever paid attention to the covers on children's Bibles? I hadn't until I had children who were receiving said Bibles as gifts. On the majority of those I've seen there is some depiction of this story. Usually it's a smiling Noah, with a long white beard, on the ark, surrounded by smiling animals, with a rainbow as a backdrop. Yet, in reality, this is a story about an extinction event. Anyone or anything not on that ark in the story met their end. That's not a kid-friendly tale. It only becomes so if we minimize the details and turn the story into a celebration of Noah's goodness or the idea that God provided a rescue for Noah and his family. That, however, fails to account for the driving factor behind the story: human violence. Stories like this would probably be rated "TV-14" if they were being broadcast on television, and it's a good idea for us to take that into consideration as we share them. Because the point isn't just the stories themselves, but it's also the meanings we take from them.

Second, this story reflects our spiritual ancestors wrestling with their own understanding of God, humanity, and the world. It represents a shift away from the way their neighbors understood the gods, which was petty and easily annoyed. They are willing to wipe out humanity because they were too noisy, after all. In the biblical account, God is grappling with how to respond to the violence of humanity. It's interesting to see how the writers of this story thought about God. We might ask, God didn't see this coming? Not according to the authors of this story. This is a great example of our forebears trying to process their experiences and ideas about God and humanity. They are making a break with the vision of the gods the surrounding cultures held and beginning to see their understanding of God take shape. This process of learning and growing happens throughout the pages of the Bible, Old and New Testament, and isn't something to be feared. It's something to be celebrated. It's also something that is still happening with us today. God is continually inviting us to learn and grow in our understanding of God. Our ancestors learned that God doesn't act out of annoyance. Perhaps we are learning that God doesn't respond to our human violence with global violence, but with love and compassion.

Additionally, I think it's important to enter into this story in its own time, listen closely to its message, and then ask what it might mean for our own time and place. Can we bridge the gap between yesterday and today in a meaningful way? When I do just that I am reminded of the old saying, "The more things change, the more they stay the same."

I recently saw a data point that stunned me. In 2021 the world spent a combined two trillion dollars on military spending. That's a two followed by twelve zeroes, friends. If budgets are moral documents, and I believe they are, what does this say about the state of the world in the twenty-first century? I can't help but be reminded of the words of Dr. Martin Luther King Jr.: "Those who love peace must learn to organize effectively as the war hawks."[1] If we want to escape the potential deluge that could undo and dis-order creation, we need a species level shift; we need a commitment to pursue peace and justice at a global scale.

The truth is that our words have power.... They can de-escalate a situation, or they can be like gasoline being poured onto a fire.

Of course, that global reality rests on the choices we all make at the individual level in our own communities and lives. Violence isn't just something that takes place on a macro level, and it isn't always physical. Rhetorical violence—the way our words can wound and impact others—is a real and serious issue. The truth is that our words have power. Just as God spoke creation into existence in Genesis chapter 1, our words have the potential to create or destroy. They can de-escalate a situation, or they can be like gasoline being poured onto a fire. Our current context, with the advent and expansion of social media, has created a kind of barrier between us and the impact of our words. We can sit behind a keyboard and type sentences that, once we hit enter, are accessible to the whole world. This is a situation that would be unfathomable to our ancestors. It also means that we can write hateful, demeaning, and dismissive things about people we have never met. We are disconnected from the impact of those words, but the recipients of them aren't. They land like a nuclear bomb, wreaking havoc on the well-being of others.

BOARDING THE ARKS

We aren't left without safe passage, however. In this story Noah and his family are provided with an ark to guide them through the Flood and into a new future. With that in mind, what might the arks available to us look like? As we live in a time of unprecedented potential for catastrophic violence on a global scale, are there opportunities for us to do things differently? Can we turn the tide and avoid our own Great Flood? Call me an optimist, but I think so.

I think the first "ark" available to us isn't something that exists outside of us, but something inside of us that we already know: empathy. How often do we see others as our enemies or as problems that we need to solve or remove? What if, instead, we allowed empathy to connect us with them at the basic level of our shared humanity? That doesn't mean there aren't people who are toxic for us. It doesn't eliminate the need to have clear boundaries, either. What it does mean is that our way forward, the path to human flourishing, is to see the humanity of others. Empathy allows us to place ourselves in another's shoes. It reminds us that, with everything that can divide or separate us, our shared humanity transcends it all. We share the human journey, and empathy places us in touch with one another's pain and experience. This practice of trying to see—really to see—the humanity of others has often surprised me, because in seeking their humanity I often encounter divinity. After all, we humans are bearing the image of the Divine, whether or not we are conscious of that reality, and perhaps what we need most is to be reminded.

Another "ark" available to us comes as a result of practicing empathy, and that is compassion. If empathy creates an awareness in us of others' experience, then compassion is what we do in response to that awareness. Think about it like this, compassion is empathy plus action.

In 2017, in North London, England, a group of people crossing a bridge noticed a man who was preparing to jump. In response these people, all strangers to him and one another, went over and held on to him to keep him from jumping. Those strangers held on to him for two hours while they waited for emergency services to arrive.[2] What would cause complete strangers to bail on their plans or be late to work to help a complete stranger? Empathy, understanding what it would be like to be in his shoes, and compassion, acting out of that shared human experience.

Finally, if we long for a better world and future on this planet, then we must board the "arks" of peace and justice. I place these two together because they are two sides of a coin; one cannot exist without the other. This became clear to me in the aftermath of George Floyd's murder in 2020. Several people from our church participated in a march calling for justice for George Floyd, Breonna Taylor, and other victims of police brutality. One of the familiar refrains we chanted as we walked was "No justice, no peace." This was not a threat, but the acknowledgment of a reality: real peace cannot exist outside of a just and equitable world.

Peace in the biblical tradition is not just the cessation of conflict, but the presence of wholeness. It's not just a lack of bombs, but the healing of wounds. The peace we desperately need will not come to us without a commitment to the work of justice. Peace calls us to the work of mending fences but also feeding bellies; of laying down arms but also creating access to human flourishing that is equitable. I am reminded of the words of the prophet Micah, who, in response to the question, "What does God require of us," said:

> [God] has told you, O mortal, what is good;
>   and what does the LORD require of you
> but to do justice, and to love kindness,
>   and to walk humbly with your God?
>   (Micah 6:8)

My hope is that the story of Noah and the Great Flood will remind us that our futures are all bound up together, and that through intentionally practicing empathy and compassion, while pursuing justice and peace, we can have a radically more beautiful future, together.

CHAPTER 2

A New Vision of God: The Binding of Isaac

Genesis 22:1-19

RAISING QUESTIONS

I was twenty-eight when I became a dad, and from the very first moment I held my son in my arms, I knew that this was a game changer. He was so very tiny, and so incredibly perfect. It was then and there that something like a switch was flipped inside of me. My heart, hopes, and dreams were now bound up with this little human who I would suddenly do anything to protect.

Something else happened in that hospital room, though. The experience of this little bundle of human joy completely transformed the lens through which I saw my faith and read the Bible. This became evident when I found myself reading stories like Abraham's near sacrifice of his son Isaac. The story, known as the *Akedah* in Hebrew (which means the "binding" and draws attention to Isaac, Abraham's son, being bound and placed on an altar, prepared for the divinely demanded sacrifice), raises all sorts of questions for me now: What kind of God demands the sacrifice of a beloved child? What kind of father attempts to go through with it? What do we do with such a story? How does a "grown-up" lens shift or alter the way we engage and interpret stories like this? But, first things first. If you've never read the story, I'd encourage you to pause here and give it a quick read before we continue.

TAKE YOUR SON

Our story begins with a test and a voice. This voice, belonging to God, is one Abraham has heard before. It's becoming familiar. Ten chapters earlier, back when he was known as Abram, God had first called out to him:

> Now the LORD said to Abram, "Go from your country and your kindred and your father's house to the land that I will show you. I will make of you a great nation, and I will bless you and make your name great, so that you will be a blessing. I will bless those who bless you, and the one who curses you I will curse, and in you all the families of the earth shall be blessed."
>
> (Genesis 12:1-3)

Abram's response was remarkable: "So Abram went, as the LORD had told him..." (Genesis 12:4a).

All of the twists and turns that lie ahead in his story—the births of sons, a new name, and more than a couple of bad decisions—occur because of the trust Abram places in the voice that called him to leave the familiar and the known to embark on a journey into mystery—"the land that I will show you." That setting out and leaving behind cement Abraham's place as the father of three major world religions and make him the poster-human for what faith looks like in practice for billions of people.

This time, however, the voice comes with the intent to test Abraham. Does that feel off to you? God testing people? Again, this story just raises questions for me. Doesn't God already know what we will do? Are we like mice in a lab, with God running experiments to see how we will respond in a given situation? It's even more confusing when we realize that the word being translated as "test" here can also be translated as "tempt." God tempted Abraham becomes even more troublesome, right?

This testing/tempting must have been problematic for ancient readers as well, so someone tried to explain what was happening through *midrash*. *Midrash* is a Jewish interpretation of a text that seeks to engage not only what the text says, but also creatively seeks to fill in the gaps and speak to the questions a text raises. If there's a story in the Hebrew Bible, there's likely *midrashim* to help interpret it. One example of this creative engagement with Scripture is a work of *midrash* called *Bereishit Rabbah* (literally, "Great in the Beginning"), in which the rabbis offer interpretations of the stories found in the Book of Genesis. For example, in the text of Genesis chapter 4 we are given no reason for God's acceptance of Abel's sacrifice and God's rejection of Cain's. The text simply reads:

In the course of time Cain brought to the LORD an offering of the fruit of the ground, and Abel for his part brought of the firstlings of his flock, their fat portions. And the LORD had regard for Abel and his offering, but for Cain and his offering he had no regard.
(Genesis 4:3-5a)

In *Bereishit Rabbah*, the rabbis explain that this outcome is because Cain didn't bring the first fruits of his crops, but just some of the leftover portion, while Abel brought the first of his flocks.

And Kayin (Cain) brought from the fruit of the land an offering [mincha] to God - from the leftovers, [similar to] the evil tenant that eats the first fruits and gives to the owner of the field the stunted ones. "And Hevel (Abel) brought, also he, from the first born of his sheep, and their fat."

(Bereshit Rabbah 22:51)[1]

As you can see, midrash seeks to interpret the text, to fill in the gaps that are present and to respond to the questions a passage or story might raise. Midrash isn't minor or novel; it's an ancient art form that loves Scripture and seeks to engage it seriously and creatively.

Midrash isn't minor or novel; it's an ancient art form that loves Scripture and seeks to engage it seriously and creatively.

An example of midrash in relation to the "Binding of Isaac" comes from a text known as "Jubilees." This is a mid-second century BCE work (c.160–150), and it's sometimes called "Lesser Genesis" because it tells many of the same stories with added detail.

Here's how Jubilees introduces the "Binding of Isaac":

And it came to pass...there were voices in heaven regarding Abraham, that he was faithful in all that [God] told him, and that he loved the LORD, and that in every affliction he was faithful.

And the prince Mastêmâ came and said before God, "Behold, Abraham loves Isaac his son, and he delights in him above all things else; bid him offer him as a burnt-offering on the altar,

and Thou wilt see if he will do this command, and Thou wilt
know if he is faithful in everything wherein Thou dost try him."
(Jubilees 17:15-16)[2]

Does that sound familiar? If so, it's probably because it is very similar to the prose beginning to the Book of Job. There a figure called "the Satan" (a title, not a name, meaning "the Accuser") presses God similarly about Job and the reasons for his faithfulness. In Jubilees it is Mastêmâ, which means hatred/hostility in Hebrew, who is a figure like the Satan, a member of God's court who functions as a kind of prosecuting attorney, that instigates the fateful test of Abraham. The approach of midrash, then, is to locate the test not so much with God, but with this figure who brings a charge against Abraham and questions the reason for his faithfulness.

Regardless of who or why, Abraham is called to by the voice of God, and he responds, "Here I am." That is a refrain we will hear three times in this story, twice in Abraham's response to God, and once in response to his son Isaac. This first time the command should cause us great discomfort is in Genesis 22:2:

> *"Take your son, your only son Isaac, whom you love, and go to*
> *the land of Moriah and offer him there as a burnt offering on*
> *one of the mountains that I shall show you."*
(Genesis 22:2)

That build is dramatic, isn't it? The tension mounts with each phrase: "Take your son, your only son, Isaac, whom you love..." (Which is even more obvious in the Hebrew, as Isaac's name appears at the end, not early on as in English translations.) Why does God do this? Why is the clarification of exactly who Abraham is to sacrifice needed? Once again, midrash comes to the rescue by filling in those details. The rabbis, again in *Bereishit Rabbah*, imagine the interchange between God and Abraham like this:

He [Abraham] said to Him, "I have two sons." He [God] said to him, "Your only one." He said to Him, "This one is the only son of his mother, and that one is the only son of his mother." He said to him, "Whom you love." He said to Him, "I love them both." He said to him, "Isaac."

Once the identity of the sacrifice was clear, Abraham heard a familiar command. When God first called Abram to leave home, it was to travel to the "land I will show you." Now, in this pivotal moment, the call is once again to journey to a place that God would show him. The difference between the two calls, however, is stark. The first was a call to follow and be blessed. This second is a call to offer as a human sacrifice a son who was an integral piece of the promised blessing. Yet, just like the original call, Abraham promptly obeys.

So Abraham rose early in the morning, saddled his donkey, and took two of his young men with him and his son Isaac; he cut the wood for the burnt offering and set out and went to the place in the distance that God had shown him.

(Genesis 22:3)

The language is void of emotion. Abraham seems almost stoic. He doesn't argue or resist. He doesn't ask God to reconsider, at least not in the story as we have it. He makes preparations and sets out to sacrifice his son, Isaac.

Let's pause here for a moment to think about how we feel as we process the introductory moments of this story. If you're like me, there's part of you that thinks we should be celebrating Abraham's swift obedience. After all, that's what we are supposed to do, right? Even when it's difficult or costly, we are to be obedient to God's commands. But that thought is fleeting for me and gives way to the horrific realization that Abraham is setting out to offer his child as a sacrifice. His obedience will cost him greatly, but it will cost Isaac more. If we allow ourselves to set down our "supposed to" response for just a moment, and instead we look at this story through the lens of the human experience, what does it bring up for us? Let's pay attention to how this story affects us as we proceed.

Perhaps one of the most gut-wrenching details is that Isaac unwittingly plays a role in his own horror story. Notice how the narrator, again seemingly without an ounce of emotion, matter-of-factly tells us of Isaac's participation: "Abraham took the wood of the burnt offering and laid it on his son Isaac, and he himself carried the fire and the knife. And the two of them walked on together" (Genesis 22:6).

This just feels brutal to me. Isaac carries the wood upon which his life will be offered as a sacrifice. He is conscripted into participation in his own death. Don't you wish you could warn him?

At some point he must've looked around and realized something wasn't quite right. They had all the elements for the ritual, save one. He asks his father, Abraham, a question: Where is the animal for the sacrifice?

> Isaac said to his father Abraham, "Father!" And he said, "Here I am, my son." He said, "The fire and the wood are here, but where is the lamb for a burnt offering?" Abraham said, "God himself will provide the lamb for a burnt offering, my son." And the two of them walked on together.
>
> (Genesis 22:7-8)

Am I the only one screaming, "It's you, Isaac! You need to run!"? It reminds me of those scenes in horror movies when people hear a noise outside and go out in the dark, alone, to investigate. I desperately want to stop them, because I know they are heading outside and a guy in a hockey mask will be waiting for them. Only this isn't a horror movie; it's a Bible story.

What are we to make of Abraham's response to his son? Is this, once again, an example of Abraham's great faith? Is he so confident that God will provide an animal for the ritual that he trusts deep down that there is no real danger to this son he loves? Or is Abraham trying to keep his son calm, to preemptively defuse any situation that might occur if Isaac were to really understand the full picture of what will happen to him when they reach their destination on the mountain?

A WORD OF CAUTION

Before we join them on the mountain for the climactic scene from this story, this is a good place for me to offer a word of caution for how we Christians approach, not only this story, but all stories in the Hebrew Bible. For the earliest followers of Jesus, their encounter of him exploded their boxes and categories. The entire Jesus experience caused them to challenge and reimagine their assumptions and beliefs about God, humanity, and the world. Part of the way they did that is by going back to their Scriptures to see if they could catch glimpses of Jesus that they had somehow overlooked before. So, when a New Testament writer describes something as "fulfilling" the words of a prophet or Scripture, we need to understand that no one had ever understood those passages in that way before. It was a reimagining and reinterpretation of their Scriptures to make space for the Jesus experience. What else could they have done? How else could they have processed such a boundary breaking experience?

The caution is that we don't begin there when we engage a story like the Akedah. Before we jump to, "What does this say about Jesus?" it's important for us to hear these stories within the context and meanings of the communities that wrote and received them. So, while many Christians have jumped immediately to how a story like this might be foreshadowing the Jesus experience, I want us to engage it first and foremost as a story about Abraham and Isaac and what our ancient spiritual ancestors might be challenging us to see.

WHAT WAS ISAAC THINKING?

Now we come to the climactic scene. The journey is over, and Abraham's faithfulness is pushed to the brink. Notice how the narrator explains the scene with language that is almost surgical, void once again, of any emotion or feeling.

> *When they came to the place that God had shown him, Abraham built an altar there and laid the wood in order. He bound his son Isaac and laid him on the altar on top of the wood. Then Abraham reached out his hand and took the knife to kill his son.*
>
> (Genesis 22:9-10)

I wonder what Isaac was thinking watching his father build an altar for a sacrifice they didn't have. Stone by stone, did Isaac start to put it all together? As the wood he had carried for this very moment was placed on the altar, did it finally dawn on him that he was the sacrifice for the ritual?

Another interesting layer is that, according to the rabbis and midrash, Isaac was somewhere around thirty-seven years old at this moment. He isn't a child! Why would a grown-up Isaac agree to place himself on the altar and lie still as his own father prepared to ritually offer him as a sacrifice?

Finally, the moment arrives. The altar is built, and the wood arranged. The sacrifice—Isaac—is in place upon the altar. Now, Abraham must do the deed. He takes the knife and begins the act of offering his son as a ritual sacrifice to fulfill the command he received from God. This translation (NRSVue), like many others, uses the word "kill" to describe what Abraham is about to do to his son; but that sanitizes the language. The actual word in Hebrew here means "to slaughter," and that does something visceral inside of us, doesn't it? It carries a weight that "kill" just doesn't quite capture.

Abraham apparently wasn't bluffing. As he prepares to plunge the knife into his son, he hears a familiar voice:

> But the angel of the LORD called to him from heaven and said, "Abraham, Abraham!" And he said, "Here I am." He said, "Do not lay your hand on the boy or do anything to him, for now I know that you fear God, since you have not withheld your son, your only son, from me." And Abraham looked up and saw a ram, caught in a thicket by its horns. Abraham went and took the ram and offered it up as a burnt offering instead of his son. So Abraham called that place "The LORD will provide," as it is said to this day, "On the mount of the LORD it shall be provided."
>
> (Genesis 22:11-14)

Just as he did in the beginning of the story, Abraham hears a voice that calls out to him. He responds, once again, "Here I am." This time, to our relief, the voice calls him not to offer his son as a sacrifice, but instead to offer a ram that was trapped in the thicket. Abraham then completed the ritual with the provided ram, and named the place where these events occurred, *Yahweh Yireh* in Hebrew, to remember the provision of that moment on that mountain.

As this story is concluded, the promise made to Abraham— that he would be blessed as the father of many, and that his family would be a blessing to the entire human family—is confirmed again. This is no doubt a pivotal moment in the story of

Abraham, but our exploration is just beginning. What does this story mean?

A NEW UNDERSTANDING EMERGES

Not long ago, my six-year-old daughter crawled into my lap with a book and asked me to read it to her, as she does often. I was immediately transported back to my childhood. The book had a white cover, and on it was a familiar image embossed in gold-foil—a young David swinging his slingshot around his head, and the giant Goliath, with his spear held back and poised for launching. Arched above that image in cursive gold letters was the title: *Bible Stories for Children*. This particular book had been a gift to me from my great-grandmother for Christmas 1982. As I snapped back into the present my daughter had opened the book to a random page and pointed to a familiar picture.

"What's this story about, Daddy?" she asked.

The image was of an old man with a long white beard, holding a knife in his outstretched arm prepared to plunge it into his son, who was bound and lying on an altar. It was the story of the *Akedah*. I was speechless for a moment, and then fortunately was able to distract her with another book. Her question, however, is the question we must wrestle with now: What does this story mean?

The meaning most readily available, which I remember being taught at a young age, is that we should all be like Abraham, willing to sacrifice whatever God calls us to in order to be faithful. If we do whatever God asks of us, then God will bless us richly as a result. That reading, however, minimizes the trauma of the story significantly. It ignores the real human experience presented in the narrative and creates an image of God that is problematic to say the least. This brings us back to the questions I raised early in this chapter.

What kind of God needs a person to prove themselves? What kind of God demands the sacrifice of a child? Even if God doesn't go through with it, the command itself is traumatic. But we can't just let Abraham off the hook. What kind of father is commanded to sacrifice his child and he just does it? Without any real protest?

To understand what might be happening in this story, we need to return to the conversation from the last chapter about sources. If you'll recall the Torah, the first five books of the Hebrew Scriptures, also called "The Law," is made up of at least four sources. We were introduced to two of them in the previous chapter, J (Yahwist, because it uses the name Yahweh for God) and P (Priestly, because it reflects the interests of the priestly class).

The *Akedah* combines the J source with a source called "E" which is short for *Elohist*, because it uses the word *Elohim* for God. *Elohim* can be a generic term for god/gods, but also in the E source it is the name by which God is known. The bulk of the *Akedah* is from the E source, with an interjection from J at a critical moment. It looks like this:

> After these things God tested Abraham. He said to him, "Abraham!" And he said, "Here I am." He said, "Take your son, your only son Isaac, whom you love, and go to the land of Moriah and offer him there as a burnt offering on one of the mountains that I shall show you." So Abraham rose early in the morning, saddled his donkey, and took two of his young men with him and his son Isaac; he cut the wood for the burnt offering and set out and went to the place in the distance that God had shown him. On the third day Abraham looked up and saw the place far away. Then Abraham said to his young men, "Stay here with the donkey; the boy and I will go over there; we will worship, and then we will come back to you." Abraham took the wood of the burnt offering and laid it on his son Isaac, and he himself carried the fire and the knife. And the two of them

walked on together. Isaac said to his father Abraham, "Father!" And he said, "Here I am, my son." He said, "The fire and the wood are here, but where is the lamb for a burnt offering?" Abraham said, "God himself will provide the lamb for a burnt offering, my son." And the two of them walked on together.

When they came to the place that God had shown him, Abraham built an altar there and laid the wood in order. He bound his son Isaac and laid him on the altar on top of the wood. Then Abraham reached out his hand and took the knife to kill his son.

(Genesis 22:1-10)

The first ten verses of Genesis 22 are from the E source, but then there is an abrupt switch. We can see that when we notice the name used for the Deity in the passage. Notice how in the first ten verses the Deity is called "God." That's the Hebrew word *Elohim*. Then, beginning with verse 11, the name shifts to *Yahweh*. You can see the change when the passage uses "the Lord" for the Deity. Lord in all caps isn't the writer shouting at us, but it's the way the Jewish tradition honors the name of God. *Yahweh* is God's personal name in the Scriptures, a name that must be honored and not taken lightly (remember the Ten Commandments?). Lord, the Hebrew word *Adonai*, is used in place of the name *Yahweh* to show reverence. So, beginning in verse 11, we encounter "the angel of the Lord," which really means *Yahweh*. The introduction of "the angel" is another way to show reverence to the Name of God.

But the angel of the Lord called to him from heaven and said, "Abraham, Abraham!" And he said, "Here I am." He said, "Do not lay your hand on the boy or do anything to him, for now I know that you fear God, since you have not withheld your son, your only son, from me." And Abraham looked up and saw a ram, caught in a thicket by its horns. Abraham went and took the ram and offered it up as a burnt offering instead of his son. So Abraham called that place "The Lord will provide," as it is said to this day, "On the mount of the Lord it shall be provided."

(Genesis 22:11-14)

As you can see, at the critical moment, when Abraham is about to slaughter his son as a ritual sacrifice, the voice calling out to him changes. The source shifts from E to J, from *Elohim* to *Yahweh*. That doesn't seem insignificant to me. Why did the editor who brought all of these sources together choose to make this shift in language? Is it possible that within this change of language we can find a meaning for this story that has often gone overlooked?

What if this story is an invitation to Abraham to experience a transformation in how he understood God? Remember, when the voice of *Elohim* called Abraham to offer his son Isaac as a sacrifice, he didn't flinch. He didn't argue, debate, or negotiate. It's almost like the command made sense to him. He immediately began making the preparations necessary to obey the command. Likewise, Isaac, even to the point of being bound and placed upon the altar, doesn't seem to protest. Is it possible that both father and son take for granted that this is just how it all works? This is just what happens; sometimes the gods demand from us the most important thing—or person—to us. The gods need us to prove how faithful we are, even when the act of proving is so costly. Abraham and Isaac don't flinch, perhaps because this isn't such an out-of-the-ordinary request, as it is for us.

When we meet Abraham, he lives in a place called Ur of the Chaldeans, which is located in modern Iraq. We aren't told much about his life before he left in Genesis, but there is an interesting line in the Book of Joshua that gives a little backstory.

Then Joshua gathered all the tribes of Israel to Shechem and summoned the elders, the heads, the judges, and the officers of Israel, and they presented themselves before God. And Joshua said to all the people, "Thus says the LORD, the God of Israel: Long ago your ancestors—Terah and his sons Abraham and Nahor—lived beyond the Euphrates and served other gods. Then I took your father Abraham from beyond the River and led him through all the land of Canaan and made his offspring many.

(Joshua 24:1-3a)

The tradition in Joshua reminds us that Abraham wasn't always the faithful monotheist he's known to be today. He began his life in a different context, with different understandings. His journey wasn't just one of geography, but one of the heart and mind. It was actually easier for his location on the map to change than it was for his understandings of God to shift.

There are moments when the invitation to us is to think differently about God.

I have come to see in this story of the near sacrifice of Isaac an invitation to Abraham, and to us, to open ourselves to changing our minds about God. Yes, you read that correctly. There are moments when the invitation to us is to think differently about God. I'm not suggesting that God changes with the times and we need to change with God. I'm saying that our understanding of God is significantly shaped by our context—where we live, what our family of origin is like, what we were taught about faith, and so much more—and we are often totally unaware of it. We assume our view of God IS God, and then operate out of that assumption. It's similar to the airplane analogy I shared earlier. We stand on the ground thinking we see everything, but when we're 35,000 feet above the ground, we can see that it's much larger and more breathtaking than we could even imagine.

The lesson Abraham learns in this story is that this God doesn't demand anything *from* him, but instead provides *for* him. In a context in which gods were demanding and ruthless, a God who cares, sees, and provides generously is a massive step forward. It seems that this is how it works in the pages of Scripture and in the experience of our lives: God meets us where we are and invites us to take a step forward. With the *Akedah* we are invited to see a trajectory that has begun, and one in which we are invited to participate and continue. What if that is one of the central goals of faith—to instigate and enable us to grow and transform? To do that we, like Abraham, must practice discerning the voice of God among all the other voices, especially those that are trying to limit and distract us.

Our participation in that moving forward doesn't come easily, however. Just like the story of Abraham, it is often the case that some experience of trauma is the catalyst that begins to open our eyes to see and understand God in new (to us) ways. Those traumatic, and potentially transformative, moments create fissures and cracks in our lenses that allow the possibility for us to see what has always been true, but what we had not yet noticed. The reality that trauma has often played a role reminds us that this trip isn't a solo expedition. We need others—friends, a therapist, a trusted community—as we navigate this experience.

Could this story be symbolic of the journey many of us have been on, a leaving behind of understandings of God that have proven too small, and an embracing of a vision of God that is more expansive, compassionate, and inclusive than we thought possible? Maybe the question for Abraham (and for us) is this: Will we leave behind the familiar and journey into the unknown?

My understanding of God has changed dramatically in my four decades plus of life, and I expect that to continue. I bet yours has and will also. From this perspective, this story isn't primitive or barbaric, or trying to freeze us in the past with an understanding of God that is traumatic and inhumane. It's actually a story of awakening that is inviting us to leave behind that image of God, in order to embrace a better one. That's still our journey. We are still about that work. We still haven't arrived. My hope is that stories like this, read through a grown-up lens, will encourage us to continue the journey, to pursue the trajectory, into the Mystery we call God.

CHAPTER 3

It's Not About the Fish: The Story of Jonah

Jonah 1–4

A WHALE OF A STORY

In the summer of 2021, Michael Packard, a lobster diver from Connecticut, had what I imagine to be an unforgettable experience. The veteran diver had just gone out for his second dip of the day, outfitted in his scuba gear, when, suddenly, he was enveloped in darkness. He quickly realized he was in the mouth of a humpback whale. The whole experience lasted thirty to forty seconds before the whale surfaced and released him back into the water.[1] Now it's a pretty incredible story to tell, but at the time it had to be pretty terrifying. Can you imagine processing the idea that you had just become human sushi? It was a near death experience of biblical proportions.

Bad puns aside, as I read the story about Packard's encounter with the humpback whale I immediately thought of the story of Jonah. It's one of the best-known stories from the Bible, and I don't think it's a stretch to say it conveys one of the central messages of Scripture. More on that in a bit. While the stories are similar, both men were briefly eaten by a sea creature, Jonah's story takes Packard's up a notch—he spent three days and nights in the belly of the great fish!

WHO WAS JONAH?

Before we sort through the details, let's begin by talking about the central character in this larger-than-life tale. Who was Jonah? What was he like? The truth is, we don't really know much. There are few biographical details in his story. The writer begins with no fluff or background. We are immediately thrust into the action of the story.

> Now the word of the LORD came to Jonah son of Amittai, saying, "Go at once to Nineveh, that great city, and cry out against it; for their wickedness has come up before me."
>
> (Jonah 1:1-2)

Based on that brief introduction, we are given three pieces of information about Jonah. First, we are given his name. *Jonah* means "dove" in Hebrew, which by the end is drenched in irony. Doves are used symbolically as an image of peace. Noah released a dove after the Flood, which brought back an olive branch. A dove descended on Jesus at his baptism, representative of the nonviolent way he would live and announce the kingdom of God. Jonah wanted nothing to do with bringing any kind of peace to Nineveh.

We are also told that his father was named Amittai (meaning "my truth") and finally that he had been given a word from God that called him to preach to the people of Nineveh. It's not a lot to go on in terms of knowing what Jonah was like. If we look outside of the book that bears his name, Jonah is only mentioned once in the rest of the Bible. He appears in passing in 2 Kings 14 in connection with Jeroboam II, who reigned as king of Israel in the eighth century BCE (786–746).

> *In the fifteenth year King Amaziah son of Jehoash of Judah,*
> *King Jeroboam son of Joash of Israel began to reign in Samaria;*
> *he reigned forty-one years. He did what was evil in the sight of*
> *the LORD; he did not depart from all the sins of Jeroboam son*
> *of Nebat, which he caused Israel to sin. He restored the border*
> *of Israel from Lebo-hamath as far as the Sea of the Arabah,*
> *According to the word of the LORD, the God of Israel, which he*
> *spoke by his servant Jonah son of Amittai, the prophet, who was*
> *from Gath-hepher.*
>
> (2 Kings 14:23-25)

Jonah is an ambiguous character, one who both knows the voice of God, and also wanted nothing to do with what God was asking him to do.

That passing reference is the only other biographical data we have about this reluctant prophet. He lived and did his work during the tenure of a wicked king, and he was from a town called Gath-hepher, which is located in northern Israel. Beyond that, there's midrash. In *Bereishit Rabbah* the rabbis propose that Jonah was the son of the widow of Zarephath. In that story, he died and was raised back to life by the prophet Elijah. What we are given in the Bible, however, is brief. Jonah is an ambiguous character, one who both knows the voice of God, and also wanted nothing to do with what God was asking him to do. Jonah didn't want to be a prophet, at least not one that went to Nineveh.

A DIFFERENT KIND OF PROPHET

It's not uncommon in the Bible for a prophet to be reluctant when called. Moses, standing on holy ground before the burning bush, offered multiple reasons why he wasn't the best choice for the job of liberator. Isaiah felt himself too impure for the task of speaking God's message to the people. Jeremiah felt like he was too young. Eventually, all of these people embraced the mantle of prophet and proclaimed the word God had given them to the people and places to which they were commissioned. Jonah, however, wasn't reluctant. He didn't drag his feet, he used them to run in the opposite direction.

> Now the word of the LORD came to Jonah son of Amittai, saying, "Go at once to Nineveh, that great city, and cry out against it, for their wickedness has come up before me." But Jonah set out to flee to Tarshish from the presence of the LORD. He went down to Joppa and found a ship going to Tarshish; so he paid his fare and went on board, to go with them to Tarshish, away from the presence of the LORD.
>
> (Jonah 1:1-3)

Tarshish was located in Spain, while Nineveh was in modern-day Syria, meaning Jonah decided to go as far away from the place he was called to go as he possibly could. It's interesting that the text says he was going "away from presence of the LORD." This was a normal understanding of how things worked in the ancient world. Deities were associated with places, and when you left that particular place and traveled into other territory, that might belong to a different god. Jonah's plan is to leave the boundaries of his God and, by doing so, avoid any repercussions that his failure to comply might generate. He was in for a surprise.

Why did Jonah run from this call to go to Nineveh? One suggestion is found in the "Chapters of Rabbi Eliezer," dated to the eighth or ninth century CE. Rabbi Eliezer relays that Jonah fled from the call to preach in Nineveh because he had obeyed an earlier command to proclaim the same message in Jerusalem. Instead of destroying the city, God was merciful and relented. Jonah's reputation was sullied, and the people began to think of him as a lying prophet. According to this midrash, Jonah fled because he didn't want a repeat of that incident.

Perhaps the reason is fairly simple: Nineveh represented a grave threat to Israel, Jonah's own country. Nineveh was the capital city of the Assyrian Empire, which dominated the landscape of ancient Mesopotamia from the late 900s to the late 600s BCE. Since they were known for the brutality with which they treated the peoples they conquered, it makes complete sense why Jonah would want nothing to do with warning them that they were on the verge of destruction. That, I'm sure, sounded fantastic to Jonah. The destruction of Nineveh, which would symbolize the destruction of the Assyrian Empire, would mean that this particular danger had passed.

Jonah wasn't wrong to be concerned about the Assyrian threat that loomed over his state. In fact, in the year 722 BCE the Israelite capital of Samaria was taken at the culmination of a three-year siege by the newly crowned Assyrian king, Sargon II. The book of 2 Kings records the aftermath of the defeat:

> Then the king of Assyria invaded all the land and came to Samaria; for three years he besieged it. In the ninth year of Hoshea, the king of Assyria captured Samaria; he carried the Israelites away to Assyria. He placed them in Halah, on the Habor, the river of Gozan, and in the cities of the Medes.
>
> (2 Kings 17:5-6)

The ten tribes that made up the Northern Kingdom of Israel were essentially lost to history. Unlike Judah in the South, that was conquered by Babylon but allowed to return and rebuild by the Persians some seventy years later, the ten tribes of the North were granted no such opportunity. Knowing all this, why would Jonah want to preach to the Ninevites? After all, his God tends toward compassion, and Jonah needs the threat eliminated. Jonah's fears, as it turns out, weren't unfounded.

OUT OF THE BOAT

Jonah's plan started off without a hitch. He went to a port city called Joppa, paid his fare, and boarded a merchant ship headed for Tarshish. Then the sea became choppy, and the clouds grew dark. The sky began to thunder. Jonah couldn't escape God after all.

> But the LORD hurled a great wind upon the sea, and such a mighty storm came upon the sea that the ship threatened to break up. Then the sailors were afraid, and each cried to his god. They threw the cargo that was in the ship into the sea, to lighten it for them. Jonah, meanwhile, had gone down into the hold of the ship and had lain down and was fast asleep.
>
> (Jonah 1:4-5)

The sailors awaken Jonah, and by casting lots determine that he is the source of the storm that is threatening all of their lives. In that moment Jonah decides to come clean with the unwitting sailors. Though they are reluctant, Jonah convinced them that if they would throw him overboard the storm would calm, and they would be safe.

> So they picked Jonah up and threw him into the sea, and the sea ceased from its raging. Then the men feared the LORD even more, and they offered a sacrifice to the LORD and made vows.
>
> (Jonah 1:15-16)

File this moment away, because it will come up again later. The Book of Jonah in more than one place is going to flip the script, in that the person you would expect to get it, to do the right, faithful thing doesn't (Jonah), and those you'd expect not to get it actually do the faithful thing (the sailors).

Jonah's well-laid plan was firmly headed south, quite literally. There's a continual downward-spiral detailed in the text. The farther Jonah tries to run, the farther down he goes.

- Jonah set out to flee to Tarshish from the presence of the LORD. He went down to Joppa and found a ship going to Tarshish (1:3).
- Jonah...had gone down into the hold of the ship and had lain down and was fast asleep (1:5b).
- So they [the sailors] picked Jonah up and threw him into the sea, and the sea ceased from its raging (1:15).
- But the LORD provided a large fish to swallow up Jonah, and Jonah was in the belly of the fish for three days and three nights (1:17).

In Hebrew editions of the Bible, chapter 1 ends with the sailors making their sacrifice to God, and chapter 2 begins with Jonah in the belly of the fish; while texts found in Christian editions include Jonah's fate as fish food.

Before we move on, a bit about the fish. The story is often told with a whale gobbling up Jonah, but that's not actually the case. The creature is called a *dag* in Hebrew, which just means "fish," and it's paired with the adjective *gadol,* which means "great." So, think of a fish. Now imagine it bigger. Keep going. Large enough for Jonah to hang out in its belly for three days and nights. That is quite the fish!

One other fish fun fact before we move on: The gender of the fish changes in the story. In chapter 1 the fish is called a *dag,* as mentioned above. *Dag* is the masculine form of the noun. Then, in chapter 2 verse 1, there is a shift to calling the creature a *dagah*, which is the feminine form of the noun. By the end of chapter 2, the fish that vomits Jonah onto dry land is once again a *dag*. What is happening here?

According to the *Jewish Encyclopedia*, midrash explains this shift in the fish's gender as follows:

> "Thus he [Jonah] spent three days and three nights in the belly of the fish, but would not pray. God then resolved to put him into another fish where he would be less comfortable. A female fish quick with young approached the male fish in which Jonah was, threatening to devour both unless Jonah were transferred to her, and announcing her divine orders to that effect...then Jonah was ejected from one fish into the over-filled belly of the other. Cramped for room and otherwise made miserable, Jonah finally prayed, acknowledging the futility of his efforts to escape from God...."[2]

That prayer is found in chapter 2, but most scholars think this is actually a psalm of thanksgiving that previously existed and was placed here into the text of Jonah. The main reason for this theory is that the prayer as we have it is not a prayer of repentance, agreeing to do what God had asked of him, but a prayer of thanksgiving for deliverance. Either way, Jonah is soon back on dry land and headed toward Nineveh.

A NINEVITE REVIVAL

Finally, Jonah set out toward Nineveh to preach a message of warning to his enemies. As I think of this sermon, I can't help but imagine Jonah speaking in a whisper, through gritted teeth.

The word of the Lord came to Jonah a second time, saying, "Get up, go to Nineveh, that great city, and proclaim to it the message that I tell you." So Jonah set out and went to Nineveh, according to the word of the LORD. Now Nineveh was an exceedingly large city, a three days' walk across. Jonah began to go into the city, going a day's walk. And he cried out, "Forty days more, and Nineveh shall be overthrown!" And the people of Nineveh believed God; they proclaimed a fast, and everyone, great and small, put on sackcloth.

(Jonah 3:1-5)

Apparently, the willingness of the preacher didn't impact the message. The response was fast and enthusiastic; every person in Nineveh, including the animal life, took Jonah's warning to heart and turned toward God in repentance. This picks up the theme I referenced earlier, about how in the Book of Jonah it's the unlikeliest—people and animals—who actually get what is going on and respond appropriately, and not those we'd imagine (like the prophet of God, Jonah).

In the Book of Jonah it's the unlikeliest– people and animals–who actually get what is going on and respond appropriately, and not those we'd imagine (like the prophet of God, Jonah).

God responded to the new situation in Nineveh by extending compassion and mercy. Nineveh would no longer be on the chopping block. "When God saw what they did, how they turned from their evil ways, God changed his mind about the calamity that he had said he would bring upon them, and he did not do it" (Jonah 3:10).

IS YOUR ANGER A GOOD THING?

It would seem that maybe that was God's plan all along. At least that's what Jonah thought. Most preachers can only dream of the results Jonah's half-hearted sermon created. An entire country responds by changing their minds and embracing the God Jonah had proclaimed to them. He didn't have to twist arms or talk them into it. No fifteen verses of "Just as I Am," either. In fewer than ten words, the people were convinced that they needed to change, and Jonah was not happy about it in the least.

> But this was very displeasing to Jonah, and he became angry. He prayed to the LORD and said, "O LORD! Is not this what I said while I was still in my own country? That is why I fled to Tarshish at the beginning, for I knew that you are a gracious and merciful God, slow to anger, abounding in steadfast love, and relenting from punishing. And now, O LORD, please take my life from me, for it is better for me to die than to live."
>
> (Jonah 4:1-3)

The truth comes out. Jonah resisted the call to preach in Nineveh because he knew in his bones that God wouldn't destroy them. He knew that God is brimming with love and compassion and that would be true even for his enemies, the Ninevites. For Jonah, this means the writing is on the wall. Why not die now and get it over with, instead of waiting around for the Assyrians? Jonah was boiling with anger.

> And the LORD said, "Is it right for you to be angry?" Then Jonah went out of the city and sat down east of the city and made a booth for himself there. He sat under it in the shade, waiting to see what would become of the city.
>
> (Jonah 4:4-5)

You have to give Jonah this, he doesn't give up easily. He stomps out of the city like a child having a tantrum, holding his breath and waiting for God to give in to his demands. The detail about moving "east of the city" is interesting. Eastward movement in the Bible is never a good thing. When Adam and Eve were expelled from Eden, they went east. Their son Cain went further east after he murdered his brother, Abel. As humans continued the eastward movement, they began to build a city with a tower that attempted to reach the sky. East, in the Bible, is away from our true humanity, away from human flourishing and being all that we were made to be. Jonah is firmly headed east, isn't he?

THE LORD PROVIDES

While Jonah waited, hoping that God would destroy the city, the sun must've been beating down on him so intently that his makeshift shelter could no longer keep him comfortable. So, God provided.

> The LORD God appointed a bush and made it come up over Jonah, to give shade over his head, to save him from his discomfort, so Jonah was very happy about the bush. But when dawn came up the next day, God appointed a worm that attacked the bush, so that it withered. When the sun rose, God prepared a sultry east wind, and the sun beat down on the head of Jonah so that he was faint and asked that he might die. He said, "It is better for me to die than to live."
>
> (Jonah 4:6-8)

God provided…a bush, a worm to eat the bush, a sultry east wind, and some sunshine. I think we are supposed to find some of this comical. Not to mention that God has already provided a great fish to give Jonah an unforgettable cruise experience. After all this provision, Jonah was ready to call it quits. He meant it this time. He was ready to leave this world. God asked him again about the anger he was nursing.

> God said to Jonah, "Is it right for you to be angry about the bush?" And he said, "Yes, angry enough to die." Then the LORD said, "You are concerned about the bush, for which you did not labor and which you did not grow; it came into being in a night and perished in a night. And should I not be concerned about Nineveh, that great city, in which there are more than a hundred and twenty thousand people who do not know their right hand from their left, and also many animals?"
>
> (Jonah 4:9-11)

Believe it or not, that's where the story ends, with Jonah east of the city, sunburned and fuming, and with God making the case for why Nineveh—and its animals—mattered. There is no resolution or conclusion. While there is comedy, this is no sitcom that will be neatly and nicely wrapped up with a bow in thirty minutes. It's almost like the author of this story, whoever he or she might have been, constructed the whole narrative to get us to this moment, to ask us this question about what God is actually like.

This larger-than-life story is contained in only forty-eight verses. In forty-eight verses we've watched Jonah run from God only to find out God was wherever he went, spend some time in a fish's belly, and be vomited out. We've seen Jonah change his direction, but not his heart. He felt the same way about Nineveh and God's call to go there in chapter 4 as he did in chapter 1 after all. Perhaps his hatred of the Ninevites was even more intense after having all that uninterrupted time to think about it. What do we do with this story? What might it mean through a grown-up lens?

Before we engage that question, let me begin by saying that the truth and power of this story does not rest in whether or not a human being was actually swallowed by a fish and subsequently spent three days and nights living in said fish. Many times, we get stuck on the detail of stories like this, did it or did it not happen, literally, and we never move beyond that to the conversation about what it might mean. So, wherever you land on that is fine with me. I want to invite you to join me beyond the literal level of the text, and into what the text is inviting us, begging us, to see.

A CENTRAL NARRATIVE

At the beginning of this chapter, I said that I think the story of Jonah conveys one of the central messages of the Bible. Let's unpack that now. I think the point the Book of Jonah is making has to do with how we see God, ourselves, and our relationship to our enemies.

When Jonah boarded the boat to head in the opposite direction of Nineveh, he assumed that would mean he was not only getting away from his enemies, but also that he was getting away from God. Yet, to Jonah's surprise, God was bigger than he imagined. This God has a universal reach.

There are essentially two kinds of prophets, or two approaches/ visions prophets in the Bible have of God and the world. The first is a nationalist approach. That's where Jonah fits. The nationalist vision is an us against the world, God is going to destroy our enemies, and we will come out on top kind of vision. Another example of a prophet who shared this vision is Obadiah. In his short book, comprised of only twenty-one verses, he envisions a time when God would help Israel (Jacob/Joseph in the text below) and destroy its enemies, in this case Edom (Esau in the following text).

The house of Jacob shall be a fire,
the house of Joseph a flame,
and the house of Esau stubble;
they shall burn them and consume them,
and there shall be no survivor of the house of Esau,
for the LORD has spoken.

(Obadiah 18)

Such is the vision of a nationalist prophet.

In contrast to the nationalist vision held by some prophets, others held a universal vision. For these prophets, God would, in the end, bring peace on earth, embracing all nations. This vision was not one of victory, but one of real, lasting, healing peace.

This is what Isaiah, Amoz's son, saw concerning Judah and Jerusalem.

In days to come
the mountain of the LORD's house
shall be established as the highest of the mountains
and shall be raised above the hills;
all the nations shall stream to it.
Many peoples shall come and say,
"Come, let us go up to the mountain of the LORD,
to the house of the God of Jacob,
that he may teach us his ways
and that we may walk in his paths."
For out of Zion shall go forth instruction
and the word of the LORD from Jerusalem.
He shall judge between the nations
and shall arbitrate for many peoples;
they shall beat their swords into ploughshares
and their spears into pruning-hooks;
nation shall not lift up sword against nation;
neither shall they learn war any more.

(Isaiah 2:2-4)

This is the vision presented in the Book of Jonah. In the end God cares for the Ninevites, just as God cares for Jonah and Israel. Jonah was invited to be part of the process through which God would call and transform Israel's (and Jonah's) enemies.

A universal understanding of God, one in which God's love is boundless for everyone and everything, also changes how we see our responsibility in the world.

A universal understanding of God, one in which God's love is boundless for everyone and everything, also changes how we see our responsibility in the world. Through Jonah's nationalist lens he had one responsibility: to his own people, Israel. If the surrounding nations, especially Nineveh, and by extension Assyria, were destroyed, this would be a cause for celebration. The author of Jonah uses him as a foil, a character in contrast, to demonstrate the immense largeness of God's love, even for those we would deny, exclude, and erase.

What if the Ninevites were to change their hearts and minds? What if they abandoned their brutality and their desire to, by force, absorb the nations around them? How would that be possible? It isn't, unless someone invites them. Through Jonah, even begrudgingly, God invites them into that experience and process.

Historically we know that this didn't happen. Assyria didn't abandon their brutality. In the year 722 BCE they conquered and absorbed the Northern Kingdom of Israel. The Book of Jonah was written after this time, probably in the fifth to fourth centuries BCE. Not only had Israel been conquered by the time of its writing, but

Nineveh itself had fallen. In the year 612 BCE the Assyrian Empire fell to the new kid on the world stage, Babylon. Why tell a story of two conquered kingdoms? What better vehicles could there be to tell a story of "what might have been" and invites us to imagine a different "what could be"? The Book of Jonah calls us to see not just our own people—religion, nation, and so on—as worthy of love and care, but all humans, everywhere. It invites us to see our species, not just our group, as our responsibility. As John Wesley put it, "The world is our parish."

I thought about how ridiculous it is, the way we carve up the world, when I was recently on an airplane. I usually fly Southwest because it's more affordable. If you've ever flown Southwest, you know there is no first-class seating. There's no assigned seating, period. You get a boarding number based on when you checked in for the flight, and then it's a free-for-all. On this particular flight I was on a different airline, and just before we took off one of the flight attendants released this mesh, see-through curtain that suddenly divided the plane. Those on the front side of the curtain received a hot towel, premium snacks and beverages, and I am sure a sense of sophistication that was absent for those of us on the backside of the curtain. The rest of us still were served, but the options were definitely different. In the moment, I couldn't help but laugh to myself. If that plane were to crash, we would all crash together.

Maybe that is what Jonah is trying show us. That regardless of where we live, what our religion is, who we love, how we vote, or any number of other things that make us different, we all share the same planet. Our success or failure as a species is intricately connected. No matter how badly we might want to, we can't escape our shared existence on planet Earth.

Which means realizing the universal love of God and our responsibility to our species calls us one step further: to rethink how we respond to our enemies. Don't get me wrong, some people are toxic to us, and we need clear and strong boundaries to protect us. That is absolutely true. God's love does not call anyone to remain in abusive and harmful relationships. What I believe the love of God does call us to is a different way of having enemies.

If we continue spending our time and creative energy trying to destroy our enemies, whether that is with bombs or social media takedowns, we will end up destroying ourselves, as well. We ultimately don't get to decide if we have enemies. Even if we decide that no one is our enemy, others might end up seeing us through that lens. What we always get to decide is how we will be an enemy.

AN OPEN-ENDED ENDING

When a movie ends without tying up all the loose ends it can be frustrating, can't it? After spending two or so hours getting invested in the characters and the story, an abrupt, inconclusive ending can be downright frustrating. That's one way to see it, at least. There is another perspective. The open-endedness is also an invitation to creativity, to engage the meaning-making process and decide how we would end the story.

Jonah has just this kind of ending. After all that Jonah had been through, from the depths of a fish's belly to the heart of Nineveh, his heart had not softened. So, as he sat east of the city, wishing and hoping for its (well-deserved, in his mind) destruction, God speaks to him one final time.

God said to Jonah, "Is it right for you to be angry about the bush?" And he said, "Yes, angry enough to die." Then *the LORD said, "You are concerned about the bush, for which you did not labor and which you did not grow; it came into being in a night and perished in a night. And should I not be concerned about Nineveh, that great city, in which there are more than a hundred and twenty thousand people who do not know their right hand from their left, and also many animals?"*

(Jonah 4:9-11)

The words *"are concerned about"* in this passage literally mean "have compassion." God says to Jonah, "You have compassion for this plant, which you didn't create, how can I not have compassion on the people and animals of Nineveh, which I did create."

Then, fade to black.

The story ends, abruptly.

All we are left with are the questions raised. Will we participate in petty back-and-forth passive aggression? Will we seek to have the last word or to cause harm? Will we hate our enemies to our own destruction? Will we be swallowed up by hate and bigotry? Will we experience the self-induced exile that refusing to seek peace and understanding will lead to?

The Book of Jonah leaves that to us to decide.

CHAPTER 4

Jesus in Unexpected Places: The Parable of the Talents

Matthew 25:14-30

THE STORIES WE TELL

My maternal grandpa was quite the storyteller. He would tell me all the standard stories that people usually tell kids (Goldilocks and the Three Bears, The Three Little Pigs, and more), but each time he would keep my attention by providing a twist. He would start with the story as usual, but then, along the way, he would shift the details and add surprising turns. He would be telling well-known stories, but his improvisation allowed them to be brand new each time. I absolutely loved story time with my Pop, because even the familiar would become new and exciting.

Humans tell stories. It seems we are wired to craft narratives that allow us to express the inexpressible. It's just in our DNA. When we gather—over a meal, for a holiday, on a road trip, or pretty much anything else we do—we find ourselves engaged in the ancient art of story. It's no surprise, then, that when we want to communicate large or complex ideas we turn to the art of storytelling. What could be more large or complex than God's dream for the world?

According to the Gospels of the New Testament, Jesus was a prolific storyteller in his own right. He regularly taught in a kind of story called parables, narratives that invited hearers to grapple with the challenge and vision he was offering them. It seems that these parables were the main vehicle through which Jesus communicated his teaching with the crowds that gathered around him:

> *With many such parables he spoke the word to them as they were able to hear it; he did not speak to them except in parables, but he explained everything in private to his disciples.*
>
> *(Mark 4:33-34)*

Some of Jesus's most memorable teachings come to us through his stories. Characters like the prodigal son and the good Samaritan are so popularly known that they have made their way into our everyday language. These stories are full of meaning, and we should take Mark's aside here as a clue for how we approach them. It seems it can be easy to miss the meaning Jesus is inviting us to engage.

HEAVENLY STORIES WITH EARTHLY MEANINGS

Before we examine one of Jesus's well-known parables, let's talk about what kind of stories they are, and what Jesus is doing with them. The English word *parable* is a transliteration of the Greek word *parabola*, which means "to cast alongside." Essentially, it's the placing of two things side by side for comparison. Sort of like, "If you can understand this, then this other thing is really similar to that." If you've been around church for a minute, you've probably heard that a parable is "an earthly story with a heavenly meaning." I'd actually like to flip those two around. I think, for Jesus, parables were heavenly stories with earthly meanings. Jesus told parables to give his listeners a glimpse into, and an understanding of, the kingdom of God. They were designed to spark the imagination, inspire curiosity, and challenge our assumptions about what is possible. Here's what I mean: Jesus uses parables to describe the kingdom of God, what it is like, and how it interacts with the world. That seems to be the key to the parables, they describe the vision that Jesus seeks to bring to bear on the world (a reality of justice, peace, compassion, and equity) by comparing it with something people would understand from their own lives or experience.

Parables were heavenly stories with earthly meanings.... They were designed to spark the imagination, inspire curiosity, and challenge our assumptions about what is possible.

A brief note: In Matthew, where our story is found, the phrase kingdom of heaven will be used. This isn't a reference to "going to heaven when you die," nor is it commentary on what heaven is or will be like. It's simply the way the author of Matthew, likely a Jewish person who followed Jesus, honors the tradition of not speaking or writing the name of God. To reverence the Name, the writer chose to use the word *heaven* instead. This isn't out of the ordinary for us. When the news is sharing information about something the president has said, they will sometimes use the name of the president ("The Biden administration released a statement…"), but other times they will use the location in which the president resides ("The White House said" or "Washington said"). They are interchangeable.

Here are a few examples from Jesus's parables, just from Matthew's Gospel:

- He put before them another parable: "The kingdom of heaven is like a mustard seed that someone took and sowed in his field" (Matthew 13:31).
- He told them another parable: "The kingdom of heaven is like yeast that a woman took and mixed in with three measures of flour until all of it was leavened" (Matthew 13:33).
- "The kingdom of heaven is like treasure hidden in a field, which a man found and reburied; then in his joy he goes and sells all that he has and buys that field" (Matthew 13:44).
- "Again, the kingdom of heaven is like a merchant in search of fine pearls" (Matthew 13:45).
- "Again, the kingdom of heaven is like a net that was thrown into the sea and caught fish of every kind" (Matthew 13:47).
- "For the kingdom of heaven is like a landowner who went out early in the morning to hire laborers for his vineyard" (Matthew 20:1).

Each of these parables is an invitation to see and embrace the challenge of the Kingdom vision Jesus announced and embodied. By using everyday images and experiences that would have been familiar to his audience, parables created an opportunity to imagine new possibilities for what the world could become. As it turns out, parables are all about possibility. They never announce what will be, but are instead invitations into, or at times warnings of, what could be.

AN INVITATION TO UNFAMILIARITY

Familiarity has the potential to create unfamiliarity. It's possible that we can be so used to something that we stop paying attention to it, and start assuming we've got it all figured out, that there is nothing unexpected left to be discovered. There are always surprises left, aren't there? People can be married for forty years and still catch one another off guard. Friends can spend decades together and still manage to offer something new that we never saw coming. I think this is also, maybe especially, true about the Bible.

Most of us were taught to read the Bible through a particular lens, and so we have. If you were raised in church like me, you probably feel like you know the stories of the Bible like the back of your hand or your own name. You might even feel like there aren't many aha moments or plot twists left. After all, the stories don't change, right? The characters are the characters, and the plot is the plot. What could be different?

I'll never forget the first time I watched the movie *Grease* as an adult. I can remember my parents watching it when I was a kid, and we even owned the soundtrack. But let me tell you, the first time I paid attention to it as a grown-up, with all the knowledge that brings, I was stunned. I had no idea how, let's say, adult some of the content of that movie actually is. This same experience can happen to us with the stories of the Bible. When we hear them in their context, we suddenly become aware of all sorts of details and meanings that were missed before. My hope is that you've already encountered that experience in this book, that new information about the context of these stories has given you a new lens and understanding of what they meant to the communities that first produced them and encountered them as sacred, and what they might mean to us today.

So, as we prepare to hear and engage the words of one of Jesus's parables, I want to ask you to do something counterintuitive. Our initial impulse is to just go with the reading that is familiar and obvious to us. We know who the God/Jesus character in the story is, for example, so we just go with that understanding. I'm going to ask that you set aside, as best you can, all of your preconceived ideas and interpretations about this story. Try to read it as if for the first time. Bring curiosity, not assumption. If we can do that, I think you might be surprised about what we find in this story and excited about the implications for other parables as well.

One final detail before we move on: The parable we are going to explore in this chapter is often called "The Parable of the Talents." Jesus didn't give his parables titles; that is something that has emerged over the centuries as people have talked about these stories. In this particular parable a talent isn't referring to a gift or ability one has, though that meaning of the word was derived from this story in the fifteenth century. A talent was both a unit of weight (80 lbs.) and a unit of currency, which was worth a lot of money—somewhere around 6,000 denarii. A denarius was the equivalent of a day's wage for a laborer. One talent was worth 6,000 day's wages. That's more than 16 year's pay. Note that for later when we hear how many talents are being thrown around by the wealthy master in this story. In the translation I am using here (The Common English Bible) the phrase *valuable coins* is used instead of *talents*, but they both refer to this unit of weight/amount.

SETTING THE SCENE

Our parable occurs within a specific context in Matthew's Gospel and seeing and understanding that context is essential for hearing Jesus's Kingdom message through it. Specifically, there are two important details that will frame our approach to the parable. First, Jesus tells this story during what Christians liturgically call "Holy Week." This is the final, climactic week of Jesus's life and ministry that begins on Palm Sunday with a peace march into Jerusalem and ends with Jesus's execution by Rome. The tension and conflict of that week isn't incidental, it is the backdrop upon which Matthew is crafting his story.

Second, our parable occurs as part of an apocalyptic warning that Jesus shares with his disciples. Notice this exchange that occurs just after a contentious encounter between Jesus and the Temple authorities.

> Now Jesus left the temple and was going away. His disciples came to point out to him the temple buildings. He responded, "Do you see all these things? I assure that no stone will be left on another. Everything will be demolished."
>
> (Matthew 24:1-2, CEB)

It's common in the tradition I grew up in to read the section this introduces as a prediction of the "end times." That isn't the case, however. Jesus is referring to a possibility that was in his disciples' immediate future, but in our ancient past. In the year 66 CE, three decades after Jesus's life, the Jewish war against Rome began, and four years later, in 70 CE, Rome had demolished Jerusalem including the Temple. That fate is what Jesus is warning his disciples about—the result of choosing the path of violent resistance against Rome. Jesus's movement was committed to resisting the brutality of the empire, but not by the use of violence. Instead, the Kingdom movement Jesus led practiced resistance through creative nonviolence. That reality is evidenced by what happened in the aftermath of Jesus's arrest and execution. The Roman authorities did not round up and execute his followers, which would have been the case if they were engaging in violent revolt.

After this apocalyptic warning, Jesus then begins to tell a series of stories, including the parable of the talents, that focus on the theme of preparedness for what is coming and what all this means for his work and the kingdom of God. Within the context of Holy Week, can't we imagine the urgency with which these stories were told? Jesus's time is coming. The writing is on the wall. Rome will soon come for him. In response to that swirling context of chaos, he tells this story.

THE ADVANTAGED FEW

Now that we are aware of the context, and we are coming with our assumptions placed to the side as best we can, listen to how Jesus begins this parable:

"The kingdom of heaven is like a man who was leaving on a trip. He called his servants and handed his possessions over to them. To one he gave five valuable coins, and to another he gave two, and to another he gave one. He gave to each servant according to that servant's ability. Then he left on his journey."

(Matthew 25:14-15, CEB)

This situation would have been familiar to Jesus's disciples but takes some explanation for us. The economy of Jesus's world was rigged in favor of the wealthiest in society (things haven't changed all that much, have they?). Roughly 1 to 2 percent, the wealthy elites, owned by some estimates, half the land. The way they came to own so much land in a context like Judea/Israel was through economic leverage. Land, in the Jewish understanding, had been given to the people by God. The land actually belonged to God and was entrusted to the Israelites to be stewarded. Even if someone lost their land due to economic difficulties (say, they used it as collateral for a loan and it was taken when they couldn't repay it), there were provisions in the Law to have it returned to them. In fact, every fifty years there was to be an economic reset, called the Year of Jubilee. The goal was to ensure that the gap between the wealthiest and the poorest did not expand unchecked and that everyone had the opportunity to "sit under their own grapevines, and under their own fig trees" (Micah 4:4, CEB).

The economy of Jesus's world was rigged in favor of the wealthiest in society . . . Roughly 1 to 2 percent, the wealthy elites, owned by some estimates, half the land.

For a such a small percentage of the population to own so much of the land, it stands to reason that Jubilee was not being practiced. Instead, through the practice of predatory loans the wealthy few gobbled up the majority of the land. To be an artisan, like a stone mason or carpenter, in the first century is likely an indicator of that displacement from family land. The man in this parable seems to be one of these economically advantaged few.

He has massive wealth and lots to manage. Perhaps Jesus is not creating a story out of thin air. I wonder if this situation hit close to home for the son of an artisan laborer.

A TALENTED BUNCH

It's easy to see how this story led to the use of talent as a particular gifting. After all, the man in the story distributes his wealth to his managers based on their ability. In this context they weren't singers or jugglers; they were adept at taking an investment and multiplying it.

In the man's absence his servants go to work. The one that was given five valuable coins went and doubled the investment, as did the servant with two coins. The servant who was given one coin, however, tried a different approach: "But the servant who had received the one valuable coin dug a hole in the ground and buried his master's money" (Matthew 25:18, CEB).

Right away we know this response is unexpected. The other servants have set a standard of what is acceptable, and this third servant misses it by a mile. Instead of investing the coin entrusted to him, he buries it. It calls to mind the practice my wife's grandpa had of burying money in coffee cans on his property. We don't know the motive for the third servant's response yet, but we should note that it is both unexpected and more than a little curious.

If the Bible came with sound effects (and I'm a little surprised no one has done that yet) this next scene would be accompanied with a dramatic "dun, dun, duuuuuuuun:" "Now after a long time the master of those servants returned and settled accounts with them" (Matthew 25:19, CEB).

It took a while, but the master finally returned to settle up with his servants. Even the least of them had been entrusted with quite a large sum of money, and now we will learn how the master perceives their actions with it. As expected, the performance review of the first two servants is glowing.

> *"The one who had received five valuable coins came forward with five additional coins. He said, 'Master, you gave me five valuable coins. Look, I've gained five more.'*
>
> *"His master replied, 'Excellent! You are a good and faithful servant! You've been faithful over a little. I'll put you in charge of much. Come, celebrate with me.'*
>
> *"The second servant also came forward and said, 'Master, you gave me two valuable coins. Look, I've gained two more.'*
>
> *"His master replied, 'Well done! You are a good and faithful servant. You've been faithful over a little. I'll put you in charge of much. Come, celebrate with me.'"*
>
> (Matthew 25:20-23, CEB)

To say the master is happy with the return on his investment is an understatement. It should put the master's wealth into perspective when he calls the amounts entrusted to the two servants—a total of more than one hundred year's wages—"a little." Can you imagine what the "much" would be? In any case, these two servants are immediately promoted and invited to a celebration of their success. What could be more praiseworthy? It's all moving up and to the right, and that is a sign of God's blessing and pleasure, right?

Let's hold off a bit before we make that judgment.

Finally, the last servant comes to give an account of what he did with the investment the master had given him. As expected, it doesn't go well for him.

> *"Now the one who had received one valuable coin came and said, 'Master, I knew that you are a hard man. You harvest grain where you haven't sown. You gather crops where you haven't*

*spread seed. So I was afraid. And I hid my valuable coin in the
ground. Here, you have what's yours.'"*

(Matthew 25:24-25, CEB)

He comes before his master with only the single valuable
coin that had been entrusted to him, nothing more added. He
had not lost anything, but when compared to the successes of
his fellow servants, well, this looks even worse in contrast. Notice
the description of the master this servant gives. Does he seem
compassionate? Just? Does he care about those around him or
how his business practices will affect the well-being of the wider
community? It doesn't seem like it. This master isn't a lamb. He's a
wolf, and he takes what he wants, when he wants, from whomever
he wants.

I know this is a parable, but I find if we enter into it and imagine how the character might have felt that it can be helpful. I
picture this final servant, a failure compared to his coworkers,
sheepishly coming before his master. He extends a trembling
hand, containing the single coin that had been entrusted to him.
He looks down and shuffles his feet as he awaits the response. As
the master begins to speak, his booming voice causes the servant
to shudder.

*"His master replied, 'You evil and lazy servant! You knew that I
harvest grain where I haven't sown and that I gather crops where
I haven't spread seed? In that case, you should have turned my
money over to the bankers so that when I returned, you could
give me what belonged to me with interest.'"*

(Matthew 25:26-27, CEB)

I find it interesting that the master here doesn't refute the
image the servant had of him. The servant saw him as a hard and
severe man, one who doesn't take no for an answer and takes
whatever he wants. The master doesn't push back. He doesn't try

to rehabilitate his image in the least. He doubles down. He leans into the image. That's exactly who he is, and he's proud of it. He didn't get this rich and make it this far by being a "nice guy," after all. If anything, it actually makes him angrier that this lazy servant knew his character and still didn't try to somehow gain something—even if it was just interest. Unfortunately, he's going to have to make an example of this evil and lazy servant.

> *"'Therefore, take from him the valuable coin and give it to the one who has ten coins. Those who have much will receive more, and they will have more than they need. But as for those who don't have much, even the little bit they have will be taken away from them. Now take the worthless servant and throw him out into the farthest darkness.'*
>
> *"People there will be weeping and grinding their teeth."*
>
> (Matthew 25:28-30, CEB)

The master lives up to his no-nonsense reputation. He takes the coin from the servant who failed to produce and adds it to the investment portfolio of the one with ten coins. Then he announces that this is just how the world works; those who have end up with more, and those who don't lose what little bit they have. I thought about that particular line recently when some people went into a camp where some unhoused people lived in our community and trashed it. They destroyed the tents and took all of their possessions and threw them away. To the people doing the demolishing, it didn't seem like much, but in a few minutes, they had destroyed everything that other human beings had for shelter. Seems on brand for the master of this story, doesn't it?

In the end, the master evaluates the servant to be worthless. After all, if you aren't producing wealth to continue to expand the empire, what good are you? The third servant must be expelled from the master's presence and thrown into the "farthest darkness" where there is suffering and agony.

WAIT A MINUTE

For some of us, I imagine that right now we are experiencing a tension. The standard interpretation of this text is that God/Jesus is the master in this story, and we are the servants. God has given us all gifts and abilities to use for the Kingdom, and if we choose not to use them, there will be serious consequences for that choice. That's not the reading I am suggesting in this chapter. Actually, I think we've really missed the meaning of this story and the challenge it presents.

Is God like this master? Really? Does the description of the master by the third servant, which the master embraces as accurate, sound like the way Jesus described God? I don't think so. When Jesus described his understanding of God, specifically what God is like in relationship to human beings, he used, not the language of abuse and punishment, but the language of care and love. For example, in his teaching about responding to our enemies, Jesus uses God as the example for our own approach:

> "Instead, love your enemies, do good, and lend expecting nothing in return. If you do, you will have a great reward. You will be acting the way children of the Most High act, for he is kind to ungrateful and wicked people. Be compassionate just as your Father is compassionate."
>
> (Luke 6:35-36, CEB)

Let's pause to really absorb this. Jesus's understanding of God is that God is kind, even to those who are ungrateful and wicked. Even more, God's compassion is to be the template for the way we show up in the world. Compassion is about entering into the suffering of others, holding them in their pain, and even working to alleviate the source of that anguish. God, as the great model of compassion, doesn't initiate suffering and pain. In Jesus's vision of God, God is found in the binding of wounds, not in their creation.

Compassion is about entering into the suffering of others, holding them in their pain, and even working to alleviate the source of that anguish.

Needless to say, I have come to realize that the standard interpretation of this parable—an interpretation I held and preached for many years—is just wrong. It paints a portrait of God as a punisher, as one who deepens the suffering and injustice of the world. That is not the God Jesus knew. The more I dig into the context, both culturally and within Matthew's Gospel, the more I think our interpretive lens for this story has been shaped by American values. It's all about success, after all. To be faithful means to work hard and reap a reward. I don't think this story by Jesus is affirming that lens. He's actually challenging it.

The version of this story told in Luke's Gospel includes an introductory line that might illuminate the meaning of this parable for us. In Luke 19 Jesus tells a story that is similar to the one we call "The Parable of the Talents," except in this story the unit of wealth is a unit called *minas* (sixty *minas* equaled one talent). Jesus tells this story about the *minas* right before the Palm Sunday entrance into Jerusalem, and he tells it to give his disciples insight into the events that lie before them.

As they listened to this, Jesus told them another parable because he was near Jerusalem and they thought God's kingdom would appear right away. He said, "A certain man who was born into royalty went to a distant land to receive his kingdom and then return."

(Luke 19:11-12, CEB)

Before the Palm Sunday march, the expectation was growing that when they entered the Holy City of Jerusalem, the kingdom of God would appear immediately. Jesus responds with this parable as a way of preparing them for the cataclysmic events that would occur by week's end. They expected a victory, but that would not look like what they expected. Jesus would be executed by Rome, and they would experience the disorientation that always comes when our expectations crash upon the rocks of reality.

FINDING JESUS IN THE UNEXPECTED

Try this interpretation on for a moment: The master in this story isn't God. Far from it, actually. This master is more like a Caesar or Herod, or other wealthy first-century power broker that developed exorbitant wealth at the expense of the average Jewish family. This would have been obvious for those to whom Jesus told this story (and Matthew and Luke's audience).

If that's the case, then who is the Jesus figure in the story? I think it's none other than the third servant. Jesus does meet a similar fate. He goes into Jerusalem in celebration, but leaves carrying his cross to the site of execution outside the city. His refusal to accept the way Caesar had decided to run the world was met with brutal force. Jesus announced, embodied, and organized an alternative way of life called "the kingdom of God." This was not a pie in the sky, heaven when you die vision, but a concrete earthy vision. Jesus envisaged a world of justice and compassion, peace and equity, in which everyone had enough. This was an "on earth" implementation of the "in heaven" reality—God's will, and not Caesar's, being done.

Part of that vision for Jesus was to refuse to engage in an exploitative economy. That's what the third servant does in this story. He buries the coin, because he won't engage in a practice that brings harm to others, especially his fellow Jews. He's being so faithful that he won't even invest it to gain interest, because that practice was forbidden in the Law (Exodus 22:25). In a sense this third servant—the Jesus character—is acting as a whistleblower, calling out the injustice and inhumanity of the system and those who sustained it. Of course, that ends one way. The whistleblower isn't praised as a hero but disposed of like a traitor.

Following this story, Jesus's opponents began plotting his demise. This kind of thinking can't catch on, because if it were allowed to, then things might begin to change for those in power (and not in a good way). Jesus meets the fate of the third servant: thrown out where there is weeping and grinding of teeth.

WHAT DO WE DO WITH THIS STORY?

This interpretation is far more challenging for me than the "use it or lose it" interpretation I inherited. Through this lens Jesus is taking a stand against the exploitative inhumanity that empire brings into the world and inviting his followers, then and now, to take up this cross. To sum up the challenge of this parable in a sentence, I would say it is this: We must refuse to participate in the harm of others. Practically, this means living thoughtfully, embracing inconvenience when necessary to ensure the well-being of fellow humans, and using our voice, privilege, and resources to bring about a better world.

Have you ever thought about how you spend your money? I'm not talking about budgeting or being smart and thrifty. Those can all be helpful, good, and responsible. I'm talking about where the money we spend, even if it's spent wisely in terms of budget, goes. To whom it goes. Are the products we buy ethically produced? Are the makers of our clothes or coffee paid a fair, living wage? How do the companies that produce the products we buy treat the environment? Are we providing financing to those that are harming people and our planet? These are hard, challenging questions, and ones that I, to be honest, struggle with. I'm not writing from a place of having it all figured out and nailed, but from a place of hope and commitment to pursue this journey, even when it isn't comfortable or convenient.

What if we made a commitment not to allow others to be bullied or harmed in our presence? I get it, speaking up and out can be very scary. When I was a freshman in high school, I was a scrawny and awkward kid. One day we were in the locker room after P.E., and some of the more mature guys started picking on another kid. I froze. Part of me knew speaking up was the right thing to do, but the other part of me didn't want to be picked on too. Well over twenty years later, I regret the choice still.

My friend, and the founding pastor of my community, GracePointe Church, often says that if we are trying to be allies to someone, and we aren't being hit with the rocks that are thrown at them, then we aren't standing close enough. I think about that often, and it's helped inform how I show up in the world. For example, to be an ally to the LGBTQ+ community means that I will speak up and out in support of their rights and against hate and homophobia. Similarly, if I want to be an ally to the BIPOC community, then I must be willing to speak up and out against racism and white supremacy, and to work to address it in my own life. To be an ally for equality, I must be willing to challenge patriarchy and the toxic theological systems that support it.

This practice will need to be contextual. Every person and situation is unique, of course, and our responses will need to be thoughtful. I raise these to mind as a way of acknowledging that they matter to me, and that to embrace the call to refuse to participate in the harm of others, I must be willing to act in meaningful ways in solidarity. It's about acknowledging and then leveraging our privilege to bring awareness and facilitate change, and then stopping harm from occurring to other people.

Through this lens, this parable is both an explanation of what will happen to Jesus as his movement lands on Caesar's radar, and a challenge and invitation to his followers—to us—to join him in resisting the ways of harm, and to seek the flourishing of all human beings. I realize how complicated that can be, especially when the approach I am suggesting cuts against the grain of how so many of us were taught to interpret these stories. Yet, I also hope you are beginning to see that it's in this challenge and complication that we hear the message and call of Jesus toward a different way of seeing God, as the compassionate one who longs for a just world, and as a result, a more divine way to be human beings in relationship with one another. May we say yes, again and again, to this invitation!

CHAPTER 5

When Repentance Isn't Enough: Looking for Zacchaeus

Luke 19:1-10

MISSING THE POINT

When I was a kid, we attended a small Freewill Baptist Church. My grandfather was the pastor. Very little was planned ahead of time for the service each week. The goal was to allow the Spirit to guide every decision in real time. We'd go to church not knowing what songs would be sung, who would sing special music, or even how many preachers we'd hear from, or who they would be. We did know one thing: every week the kids would come up front and sing a song.

We'd sing "He's Still Working on Me," "This Little Light of Mine," "Jesus Loves Me," "the B-I-B-L-E," and so many others. One of our favorites was a song about Zacchaeus and his tree climbing adventures. The lyrics go like this:

Zacchaeus was a wee little man,
And a wee little man was he.
He climbed up in a sycamore tree
For the Lord he wanted to see.
And as the Savior passed that way
He looked up in the tree,
And he said, "Zacchaeus you come down,
For I'm going to your house today!"
For I'm going to your house today!

It didn't really occur to me as a kid, but the entire focus of that song is essentially about two things: first, Zacchaeus was on the shorter side, and second, he could climb a tree. The problem with this is that it actually draws our attention away from the point of the story. The significance of Zacchaeus isn't his height, but his response to his encounter with Jesus. I wonder why that might be the case? Why would we want to focus on something more trivial and shallower as opposed to the transformation Zacchaeus experiences as a result of his encounter with Jesus?

A PIT STOP ON THE JOURNEY TO JERUSALEM

If we zoom out from the story of Zacchaeus, we will discover that it's part of a larger narrative in Luke and Acts. Both of these texts come from the pen of the same author, and both are organized around the theme of "journey." Beginning in Luke 9:51 we find that Jesus was determined to make the journey to Jerusalem. We shouldn't think of this as a casual tourist adventure. Jesus isn't just going up as a pilgrim to celebrate the festival of Passover. Instead, think about it like a president-elect making the journey to Washington, D.C., for Inauguration Day. Arriving in Jerusalem will lead to the fateful and final encounter between Jesus and Caesar.

The values of the kingdom of God would confront and clash with the values of the empire in dramatic fashion, leaving Jesus nailed to a Roman cross. In the companion volume of Acts, the message about Jesus is carried by those belonging to "the Way"—Luke's language for the early Jesus communities—from Jerusalem to Rome. The encounter between Jesus and Zacchaeus takes place within the context of this journey theme.

Luke introduces the story by giving us a geographical context, letting us know where Jesus is on the journey to Jerusalem: "Jesus entered Jericho and was passing through town" (Luke 19:1, CEB).

Jericho might sound familiar to readers of the Bible. Many of us might remember it from the story of Joshua, a hero from the Hebrew Bible who led the Israelites on a successful conquest of the city in the book named for him (Joshua 6). It's worth noting that Jesus is the Greek version of the Hebrew name Joshua (which means "Yahweh saves/is salvation"); so we might want to pay attention to how differently Jesus—Joshua 2.0—shows up in the same village. You may also recall that one of Jesus's most well-known parables, which we call "The Good Samaritan," takes place on the path going from Jerusalem down to Jericho. Jesus was making the trek from Jericho up to Jerusalem, a distance of around seventeen to eighteen miles.

Jesus was traveling with a band of his followers and not just the Twelve. In Luke 10 we find out that there are at least seventy-two disciples tagging along with him. It also seems that in each village or town he entered he immediately drew a crowd. That isn't surprising. After all, Jesus's reputation and Kingdom message was spreading like wildfire. He was healing, exorcising, and feeding people everywhere he went. That was the Kingdom vision—a world in which everyone had access to the embrace of community, liberation from oppression, and enough to sustain their lives. In an occupied country, among an oppressed people, where the inequality grew exponentially by the day, Jesus's message would have inspired the hopes and dreams of his Jewish siblings.

MEETING ZACCHAEUS

As the Kingdom tour entered Jericho, we are introduced to this man Zacchaeus, who is far more than the one-dimensional character we've come to know through children's Sunday school songs.

> A man there named Zacchaeus, a ruler among tax collectors, was rich. He was trying to see who Jesus was, but, being a short man, he couldn't because of the crowd. So he ran ahead and climbed up a sycamore tree so he could see Jesus, who was about to pass that way.
>
> (Luke 19:2-4, CEB)

Let's begin with the name, Zacchaeus. As we've seen with Jesus/Joshua, names were loaded with significance and meaning. Zacchaeus was no exception—his name means "pure/righteous." For the original audience of Luke's Gospel, this name applied to this person would be a little ironic, to say the least. Zacchaeus was an architelones, a ruler among tax collectors. People like Zacchaeus were despised by their fellow Jews, and for good reason. Tax collectors were collaborators with the occupying Romans. Tax collectors acted as agents of the empire, enforcing their taxation policies on the already struggling populace, but it didn't stop there. While they were employed by Rome, tax collectors weren't compensated by Rome. They made their living by taking all they could, over and above the prescribed amounts.

I recently bought a ticket to a concert online, and I was shocked when I saw the final cost. The seat itself was listed as being $35, which I thought was a bargain. However, when I finally checked out, I was met with a rude awakening: there were convenience fees, order processing fees, a facility charge, and then taxes that pushed the ticket cost to over $70. That's kind of the approach tax collectors had the liberty to take. Their wealth was being accrued at the expense of their fellow Jews, a reality that created a deep-seated (and understandable) bitterness among those who were being exploited. By collaborating with Rome to fund the empire (and to line their own pockets) they were actively participating in the oppression of their own country. Which is why, early in Luke, John the Baptist calls the tax collectors coming to participate in baptism to do things differently.

> Even tax collectors came to be baptized, and they asked him, "Teacher, what should we do?" He said to them, "Collect no more than the amount prescribed for you."
>
> (Luke 3:12-13)

John's response to those tax collectors is a command to stop extorting the already pressed and squeezed populace for their own gain. Once you become aware of this reality, you can see it throughout the stories in the Gospels, especially Jesus's parables. Think about stories that involved itinerant farmers, day laborers, and debt collection. There's also the scandal of Jesus's willingness, not only to engage, but to actually eat meals with tax collectors.

> After this he went out and saw a tax collector named Levi sitting at the tax-collection station, and he said to him, "Follow me." And he got up, left everything, and followed him.
>
> Then Levi gave a great banquet for him in his house, and there was a large crowd of tax collectors and others reclining at the table with them. The Pharisees and their scribes were complaining to his disciples, saying, "Why do you eat and

drink with tax collectors and sinners?" Jesus answered them, "Those who are well have no need of a physician but those who are sick; I have not come to call the righteous but sinners to repentance."

(Luke 5:27-32)

Notice the shock, the outrage even, that Jesus, a respected teacher, would sit to eat with someone who was so problematic. Meals, after all, were much more significant experiences in the ancient world, loaded with symbolism and meaning. To eat with someone was to make a statement about belonging, about equality. Reclining at the table with someone suggested alignment or approval. Jesus's willingness to share bread and wine with a tax collector just didn't compute; they were part of the problem!

Meals were much more significant experiences in the ancient world, loaded with symbolism and meaning. To eat with someone was to make a statement about belonging, about equality.

Now all the tax collectors and sinners were coming near to listen to him. And the Pharisees and the scribes were grumbling and saying, "This fellow welcomes sinners and eats with them."

(Luke 15:1-2)

Zacchaeus was one of these tax collectors. He was both participating in and benefitting from the oppression of his own people, and at the same time, deeply curious about this Jesus and his movement. Which is how he ended up in that tree.

SEEING AND BEING SEEN

When Zacchaeus heard that Jesus was entering Jericho, he knew he had to get a glimpse of this enigmatic figure who was turning the world he knew upside down. As we've already seen, Jesus was drawing crowds everywhere he went. His words and deeds were starting to cause people to believe another world was possible—a world of justice, governed by compassion and love. This vision was actually a threat to Zacchaeus's line of work. For a modern example, think about an executive of an oil company hearing that a climate change activist was coming to town to give a presentation about the urgency of ending our dependence on fossil fuels. If too many people sign on for this, Zacchaeus's way of life could be headed for extinction.

Yet, there was just something that Zacchaeus couldn't shake. Maybe he had heard that Jesus had already recruited people from his profession, and that they'd joined him as disciples. Whatever the reason, he had to see who this person was that had everyone so energized and excited, but the crowds were making it all but impossible. Zacchaeus was, after all, a short man. Undeterred, he climbed a nearby tree to catch a glimpse of Jesus passing by. He just wanted to see Jesus. What he didn't know was that Jesus would see him. "When Jesus came to that spot, he looked up and said to him, "Zacchaeus, come down at once. I must stay in your home today" (Luke 19:5, CEB).

What must have gone through Zacchaeus's mind in that moment? I can just imagine him looking around, then the moment of slow recognition as he points to himself and asks, "Me? You're coming to my house?" It was an opportunity that Zacchaeus could not miss: "So Zacchaeus came down at once, happy to welcome Jesus" (Luke 19:6, CEB).

Zacchaeus had climbed that tree to see Jesus, but in the end, it was Zacchaeus who was seen by Jesus. In that unlikely moment, everything began to change for the tax collector from Jericho. He had been seen, not as the enemy or a sinner, but as a human.

This was surely an unexpected turn of events. Jesus chose not to eat in the home of a religious luminary or even one of his own followers. He would, instead, feast in the home of a tax collector. This wasn't a popular decision. "Everyone who saw this grumbled, saying, 'He has gone to be the guest of a sinner'" (Luke 19:7, CEB).

Everyone grumbled. That is quite a statement, isn't it? Not just those who were opposed to Jesus's movement or message. Not just those that had a disagreement with Jesus's interpretation of Scripture or vision for the world. Everyone. If I had to guess, I would say this included some of Jesus's own followers. This movement Jesus was leading was seeking to change the world, after all, and part of that meant people like Zacchaeus no longer taking advantage of people. Why wouldn't Jesus go into the home of a disciple to eat? What could be more of an honor than for a disciple to host the Teacher in his or her home for a meal? Yet, Jesus chooses to invite himself into the home of a notorious tax collector. The very food Jesus would be eating was purchased with money that was ill-gotten. Zacchaeus's entire life was supported by injustice, and in going into his home the perception must have been that Jesus was giving him a pass.

The specific frustration expressed by the grumbling "everyone" is that Jesus was allowing himself to enter the home and be the guest of a sinner, someone who is living in ways that are harmful to the community. Let's just pause for a moment to acknowledge that their concern is really valid. I don't think the "everyone" in the story represents bad, mean-spirited people.

They are people who have been harmed by the Zacchaeuses of the world, and their reluctance toward Jesus's embrace of a tax collector is valid and understandable to say the least.

JUSTICE: IT'S WHAT'S FOR DINNER

We don't have any of the details between Zacchaeus leaving his perch in the tree and Jesus coming home for dinner. What did the conversation look like? Did Zacchaeus ask questions? Did Jesus tell a parable? What was on the menu? Who else came? Luke doesn't tell us. All we get is that Jesus invited himself to dinner, Zacchaeus enthusiastically welcomed him into his home, and the impact was immediate: "Zacchaeus stopped and said to the Lord, "Look, Lord, I give half of my possessions to the poor. And if I have cheated anyone, I repay them four times as much" (Luke 19:8, CEB).

It's not even clear that they made it to Zacchaeus's house before he announced a change of heart. He stopped—literally in Greek it means to "make a stand"—and pledged to give away half of his stuff and further to repay anyone he had cheated dishonestly. There are two important points here. First, the language in Zacchaeus's announcement is not future tense, but present. He's not saying, "Over time, someday, I will donate up to half my possessions and repay those I cheated." It's more urgent than that. He's actually saying, "Today, I give half my possessions away and today, I will repay those I cheated." This isn't one of those things that we decide in an emotional moment and then forget about. Zacchaeus's experience of Jesus was so profound and powerful that he acted urgently and immediately.

Second, Zacchaeus knew his Scriptures. His reference to repaying four times what he had acquired through ill-gotten means is actually a reference to a passage in Exodus 22: "When someone steals an ox or a sheep and slaughters it or sells it, the thief shall pay five oxen for an ox and four sheep for a sheep" (Exodus 22:1).

The point of this law is that when harm has been done, the response isn't just repayment, but reparations. In this case, there is no "if" someone has been cheated. It's clear that Zacchaeus knows he's caused harm to others, and he commits to making it right by paying reparations up to four times the amount he defrauded. The encounter with Jesus transformed Zacchaeus in real and practical ways. He could no longer keep harming others and benefitting from it. The change was both urgent and emphatic, and the local community would no doubt be transformed by the return of their resources.

WHAT DOES SALVATION MEAN?

Jesus's response to Zacchaeus no doubt will mess with our theological categories. When you hear the word *salvation*, what is that comes to mind? Perhaps it's believing certain doctrines about Jesus or praying a certain prayer? In this story Jesus calls Zacchaeus's decision to give away possessions and make reparations a "salvation" experience: "Jesus said to him, ' Today, salvation has come to this household because he too is a son of Abraham. The Human One came to seek and save the lost'" (Luke 19:9-10, CEB).

Salvation, Jesus says, is the word that best describes the experience of Zacchaeus in this story. What might that mean for how we think about salvation? Is salvation essentially about having the "right" beliefs so that you can attain an optimal afterlife experience? To put it another way, is salvation primarily about forgiveness, or is salvation something more?

84

In the Bible, the central lens through which salvation is understood is that of the Exodus event. The story of God's liberation of the enslaved Hebrews is the defining narrative of the Bible. It is also a narrative that cuts against the grain of how most of us have been taught to believe God works.

In the ancient world, the understanding was that to be powerful and wealthy meant that the gods were on your side. Those in power are in their positions because the gods have willed it, and any attempt to resist their control means that you are working against, not humans, but the gods themselves. The Exodus story flips that narrative on its head. The God we meet in the Exodus is not supporting those in power, but those who are powerless. This God is a liberator.

The overarching image of salvation in the Bible is not that of forgiveness, but of liberation. When Jesus talks about salvation, as a faithful Jewish person, it stands to reason that the Exodus experience would be at the core of his understanding. From this perspective Zacchaeus's salvation experience is about being liberated from participation in a greedy and unjust system that was causing deep harm to his neighbors.

Jesus connects his own mission to that work of salvation as liberation and to "seeking and saving the lost." That language of being "lost" has often been used to describe those who aren't Christian. They are "lost" people, we were taught. I don't think that's what Jesus means here. After all, Christianity didn't even exist at this point. The word *lost* in Luke is often used to describe tax collectors and sinners—those who would have been excluded and thus forgotten. Is it possible that Jesus uses *lost* as a way of reminding his listeners that those they are excluding are still "children of Abraham" that matter and deserve belonging? Could he be calling the community to help them experience healing and transformation, not through shame and exclusion, but through love and belonging?

A WORTHY RISK

Jesus was willing to risk controversy to create an opportunity for Zacchaeus to experience liberation from his greed. Notice how he frames the experience: "Jesus said to him, 'Today, salvation has come to this household because he too is a son of Abraham. The Human One came to seek and save the lost'" (Luke 19:9-10, CEB).

Jesus saw Zacchaeus as a child of Abraham, and this entire episode was about helping Zacchaeus wake up to that truth. He doesn't suddenly become part of the family once he decides to give away his stuff. On the contrary, he's always been a child of Abraham. What Jesus does by seeing and engaging Zacchaeus not only shares that good news with the surrounding community, but also with Zacchaeus, himself. This same theme of the lost one being found occurs earlier in Luke as well, in the parable of the prodigal son (Luke 15). The son who left home, seemingly burning all the bridges on his way out, eventually comes back home having lost all of his wealth. Yet, he has always been a son. His temporary forgetting of that truth didn't mean he stopped receiving the love and care of his parent.

It seems so much of what Jesus does in the Gospels is grounded in calling people back to who they truly are.

It seems so much of what Jesus does in the Gospels is grounded in calling people back to who they truly are. It's an invitation to wake up to what has always been true about the prodigal son, Zacchaeus, and us. That coming home is not easy, to be sure. It involves difficult decisions, and it can even feel costly when the system has been good to us.

THE RICH YOUNG RULER

One of the most important pieces of this book is the reminder that every story in the Bible is part of a larger context. While we often want to single out a story and use it to make a point or to moralize, the truth is that it's part of a larger narrative to which, if we want to really connect and understand the meaning of these stories, we must pay attention. The Zacchaeus story is a fantastic example of the interconnectedness of the stories in Luke's Gospel. If we turn back a chapter, to Luke 18, we will discover an interesting progression that might help us more deeply appreciate the Zacchaeus story.

In Luke 18, after Jesus blesses a group of children, he engages a person identified as "a certain ruler." While that is a bit vague, the idea of this person being a ruler clearly means he is a person of both wealth and power. He asks Jesus a question: "Good Teacher, what must I do to inherit eternal life?" (Luke 18:18)

We must resist the urge to transform this question into, "How do I go to heaven when I die." That's not the ask here. The understanding shared widely among Jews in the first century was that there was "the present age," full of injustice and suffering, and after that, "the age to come." The "age to come" was understood to be a time of justice and peace, when things would be put right, and all would have enough. The question asked by this rich ruler was grounded in the latter, not the former. He wants to ensure that when the world is set right he has a place in that reality. Keep that in mind as we read Jesus's response.

Jesus said to him, "Why do you call me good? No one is good but God alone. You know the commandments: 'You shall not commit adultery. You shall not murder. You shall not steal. You shall not bear false witness. Honor your father and mother.' "

(Luke 18:19-20)

How can this rich ruler ensure he's part of the "age to come"? Jesus tells him to keep the commandments. The five specific commands he mentions are found in the version of the Ten Commandments found in Exodus 20 (there are two other versions, one in Exodus 34 and the other in Deuteronomy 5). If we want to break down the Ten Commandments relationally, the first four deal with the people's relationship to God, and the following six focus on how people in the community relate to one another. Jesus only lists five commands here, all of which speak to relationship on the horizontal plane. This means Jesus left out of his response one of the commands that deal with interpersonal relationships. Did he forget it? Maybe it was an accident? I don't think so. Jesus is doing brilliant Jesus things, which will become clear as the dialogue continues.

Then the ruler said, "I have kept all these since my youth" (Luke 18:21).

Let's bracket whether or not the rich ruler had, in fact, kept all of those commands since childhood. It's possible that he had. The point is that he felt confident that he'd made a good faith effort to keep the commands Jesus had listed. If that were the case, what was he lacking? What would prevent him from experiencing and participating in the "age to come"? Perhaps his question was less about what he should do, and more looking for the affirmation that he had done everything that he needed to in order to receive both Jesus's praise and a place in the remade world. Whatever his motivation, Jesus pressed further.

> *When Jesus heard this, he said to him, "There is still one thing lacking. Sell all that you own and distribute the money to the poor, and you will have treasure in heaven; then come, follow me."*
>
> *(Luke 18:22)*

See? Jesus is doing brilliant Jesus things. He leans into the conversation, hoping that the rich ruler was sincerely seeking the life of the "age to come." Now the command Jesus had previously omitted comes into focus:

> *Do not desire and try to take your neighbor's house. Do not desire and try to take your neighbor's wife, male or female servant, ox, donkey, or anything else that belongs to your neighbor.*
>
> *(Exodus 20:17, CEB)*

This is probably more familiar in this language: "Do not covet." Some commentators argue that the command being transgressed by the rich ruler is the first, having no gods before God. However, it seems more likely to me that, since Jesus raised the other human-to-human relational commandments, the command against coveting makes the most sense here. After all, in the economic world of the first century if someone had wealth there was a high likelihood that it was created and maintained at the expense of the poor. When the vast, overwhelming majority lives below a subsistence level, the reality is that amassing wealth isn't an activity that is neutral in impact.

Jesus's invitation to the rich ruler is to liquidate his assets and distribute the proceeds to the poor, and then he would gain what he was seeking—a place in the "age to come." Think about it like this, the activity that created the rich ruler's wealth was actually preventing the "age to come" from being reality. This rich ruler could not keep up business as usual if he longed for that world of justice to arrive. Jesus isn't creating a hoop for the rich ruler to jump through; he's drawing his attention to the truth that the rich man's own actions are making the world he claims to long for a present impossibility. If he were to reinvest his wealth into the community, it would go a long way toward creating the conditions for human flourishing, and that, after all, is what the "age to come" is all about.

The cost was too high for the rich ruler. The "age to come" for everyone would come at the expense of the "present age" that was working quite nicely for him. His personal comfort outweighed the potential for human flourishing. "But when he heard this, he became sad, for he was very rich" (Luke 18:23).

A TALE OF TWO RICH PEOPLE

Let's come back to the Zacchaeus story. Just a chapter apart, the author of Luke has given us two dramatically different responses to Jesus and the Kingdom vision he presented. The first, the rich ruler, was challenged to (quite literally) put his money where his mouth was. If he wanted to see the "age to come," he could get the ball rolling by divesting himself of his wealth for the benefit of his neighbors. He walked away from that opportunity saddened, but still extremely rich.

On the other hand, just a chapter later, Zacchaeus is a totally different story. Unlike the rich ruler, we aren't told of any self-justifying conversation between Zacchaeus and Jesus. There is simply the interaction when Jesus calls to Zacchaeus while he's in the tree and announces that he would be the guest of the tax collector that day. It what seems like an on-the-spot reaction, Zacchaeus begins to practice justice, giving away possessions and paying reparations to those he cheated. In Jericho, Zacchaeus's response would no doubt have made an immediate and dramatic impact. The "age to come" was bursting forth in the "present age."

FINDING OURSELVES IN THE STORY

I am continually reminded just how brilliant the Gospel writers were. Luke is weaving a narrative and asking us where we see ourselves, and perhaps where we would hope to see ourselves. Are we the rich ruler, holding so tightly to the way things are because it works for us? Or are we Zacchaeus, finding ourselves so seen and caught up in Jesus's vision for the "age to come" that we make the hard choices because we know that when our neighbors flourish, we flourish?

To be honest, these stories challenge me and make me far more uncomfortable than I'd like. It makes so much sense to me now why we spent our energy focusing on Zacchaeus's height all this time. By doing so we have been able to avoid the invitation and uncomfortable challenge of his story. The truth is I have way more in common with the rich ruler than I'd ever like to admit. If I take Jesus seriously, however, then I have to embrace not only the comfort he brings, but also the challenge and discomfort. One of the most important lessons I've learned in the tension between the rich ruler and Zacchaeus is that while I've been waiting for God do something about the world's problems, God has actually been waiting for me. Every inequity and injustice that exist on this planet is a humanly created problem, and at the same time, the solution to those problems will come from us.

God will not impose the "age to come." That's what the rich ruler learned that day. When presented with God's dream we have the freedom to choose a human nightmare instead. Yet, when we choose to collaborate with God, when we choose to acknowledge our complicity in the "present age" and the systems and injustices that are actively harming people, then a different world becomes not just possible, but more and more a reality.

WHEN REPENTANCE ISN'T ENOUGH

The word *repent* doesn't explicitly appear in the Zacchaeus story, but it's definitely the subtext undergirding his actions. To *repent* is often associated with the idea of feeling sorry, and no doubt feeling the weight of how we've treated others does play a part in the process. However, repentance is really about changing our minds. That's literally what the word means, "to think differently." Zacchaeus's encounter with Jesus leads to a dramatic shift in thinking for him, but that shift alone isn't what makes this story so compelling. Yes, Zacchaeus repents, but he also takes another step in the process: repentance leads to repair. Perhaps we could say that repentance and repair are two sides of the same coin. It's not simply embracing different information in our brains, but it's also allowing that new information to transform our hearts, which will lead to a different way of being in the world.

Repentance is really about changing our minds.

By making reparations, Zacchaeus acknowledged the harm his previous approach had caused the community and in a real, practical way he made healing for the community possible. Without the action of divesting himself of his ill-gotten gains, it would only be a partial transformation, and it would not have made a difference for those he had previously harmed. I believe this combination of repentance and repair is the necessary approach for bringing healing and transformation to the world—both individuals, communities, and countries (like the United States, where we have much work left to do in this department).

THE KINGDOM BELONGS TO SUCH AS THESE

While I have been writing these words my kids have been playing in the next room. I've been a little distracted by listening to their laughter and conversation (I hope you can't tell), with their uninhibited giggles filling the air with joy. At what seems like the perfect moment, I overheard this conversation between our six-year-old twin girls.

"Do you want to be rich when you grow up," the younger asked.

"No," the older replied, "I just want to be a normal human."

The truth is many of us have lived in a system our entire lives that has reinforced that the measure of our value and worth is what our bank accounts say. We've bought into the myth that bigger and newer is better, that having more than our neighbor means we *are* more than our neighbor. Our energy and lives have been devoted to the perpetuation of a system that harms all of us in the long run. Then we look around and wonder why the world is in shambles and what we need to do to make a different world possible.

"You know the commands," Jesus tells us.

"We're really good at obeying the rules and believing all the things," we proudly say.

"One thing you lack," Jesus continues. "Radically transform your relationship to money and stuff. Challenge the systems that protect and reward the small but powerful few and harm the many. Dream up a world where everyone has enough, and then actively make it so. Then you will know the 'age to come.'"

How will we respond? What kind of world will we build? Those are the questions the rich ruler, Zacchaeus, and we must answer.

When I think about that interaction between my kids, I can't help but remember Jesus's words in Luke 18, right before the encounter with the rich ruler.

> *People were bringing even infants to him that he might touch them, and when the disciples saw it, they sternly ordered them not to do it. But Jesus called for them and said, "Let the children come to me, and do not stop them, for it is to such as these that the kingdom of God belongs. Truly I tell you, whoever does not receive the kingdom of God as a little child will never enter it."*
> *(Luke 18:15-17)*

My kids understand that so much more easily than I do. They are more worried about being human than being rich. According to Jesus, becoming like them is what it takes to enter the Kingdom. Not because there's a bouncer at the pearly gates who will keep us out if we don't, but because the Kingdom is a here-and-now reality that we will miss if we don't begin to "see" like children do. It's not God who will keep us from it. We are the ones who will prevent ourselves (and as a result our neighbors) from entering, because the Kingdom comes as we participate in bringing it.

May the kingdom come, on earth, as it is in heaven.

May we join God in making it so.

CHAPTER 6

Updating Our Lenses: Healing the Man Who Was Blind

Mark 8:22-26

AN EVOLVING PRESCRIPTION

Every year, probably like you, I pay a visit to my optometrist. By now it's a routine experience. When they call my name I go back into the preliminary testing room, where they will shine lights into my eyes and blow that horrible, violent puff of air into each eye to measure the pressure. I can never, ever do that test on the first try. After that initial assessment they move me to an exam room, invite me to sit in a chair and cover each eye in turn, and tell me to read the smallest line of letters that I can make out. Then, after what is usually a brief wait, the doctor comes in to conduct my exam.

This is the part I find so fascinating. He pulls down this butterfly looking contraption that has two sides that each contain multiple lenses. Then he asks the following question, "Which is more clear? Number one or number two?" Then he flips the next two lenses, and we keep going until he has an understanding of how I am seeing. The whole exam is a process of the doctor helping me discover what prescription will allow me to see most clearly and sharply. I go through this experience yearly because my vision can (and often does) change over the course of time. What once seemed clear, after a couple of years, can gradually become blurry. It's not that the doctor doesn't know what he's doing or is somehow failing to get it right. A prescription must keep evolving and my vision changes in order to help me see in the best possible way.

SEEING THE SIGNS

In this chapter we are going to look at one of the many stories of Jesus doing what we often call a "miracle." On page after page of the Gospels we find Jesus healing the sick, raising the dead, exerting power over nature, and exorcising unclean spirits. It's often said that Jesus performed these powerful deeds as a way of showing who he was to the world—that he was God in human skin. From this perspective, the point of such miracles is that they happened—that Jesus did them and through them offered proof of his divinity. What if, however, that understanding caused us to miss the larger meaning behind what we call the "miraculous" works of Jesus?

In the Gospel of John, the writer uses a specific designation for Jesus's actions that transcend the ordinary; he calls them "signs." I find this to be extraordinarily helpful to keep in mind when I am engaging stories like the one we are looking at from Mark chapter 8. Jesus's healing action isn't just about the restoring of sight to a man who was blind. It's actually a sign that is attempting to draw our attention somewhere. Because that's what signs do, right? Signs point, they direct. Imagine you're driving down the highway and you see a sign with an arrow pointing toward the right. It reads: "Nashville 15 miles." Your impulse isn't to stop the car and just stare at the sign. You don't assume the sign is the destination. Actually, you could spend all your time looking at and admiring the sign and never be any closer to Nashville. The point is to understand where the sign is directing you and then follow where it leads.

A dear friend of mine recently told me about an experience he had when he was invited to an Easter play at a church in his community. He said the entire play focused on the miracles of Jesus—one scene after another of healings and exorcisms. Then, he noted, abruptly Jesus was arrested and crucified. He described it as a kind of whiplash and was left wondering what those miracles had to do with anything, especially Jesus's death. After all, why would anyone be upset that someone had the power to heal and do other powerful deeds? This is why the idea of signs matters. If we see these signs, really SEE them, they will always point beyond themselves to the larger mission and message of Jesus. Let's keep this in mind as we begin to explore Jesus's healing of a man who was blind in Mark chapter 8.

Like most of the stories found in the Gospels the encounter between Jesus and this man happens while Jesus is on the move. That is especially true in Mark. Being the shortest Gospel, the writer doesn't waste any time. Jesus is on the move from the word go: "[Jesus and his disciples] came to Bethsaida. Some people brought a blind man to him and begged him to touch him" (Mark 8:22).

Bethsaida literally means "house of fisherman," and according to John's Gospel it was the hometown of Simon Peter, one of

Jesus's most well-known-to-us disciples. In this particular episode, "some people" are the instigators of the healing experience. This isn't the first time in Mark an anonymous group helped facilitate an encounter with Jesus. In chapter 2 we find a similar set of circumstances:

> When he returned to Capernaum after some days, it was reported that he was at home. So many gathered around that there was no longer room for them, not even in front of the door, and he was speaking the word to them. Then some people came, bringing to him a paralyzed man, carried by four of them. And when they could not bring him to Jesus because of the crowd, they removed the roof above him, and after having dug through it, they let down the mat on which the paralytic lay.
>
> (Mark 2:1-4)

In both of these texts, community plays a key role in the outcome of the experience. It's through the love and care of friends that both of these people encounter Jesus and become caught up in the story that's unfolding through him. Isn't that the point of being part of a community? When I was in seminary, I took an anthropology course that began each class with a student-led reflection. One particular meeting stands out for me, and I will never forget it. The student leading shared about a time in their journey when they were struggling through some challenges, and it had been so difficult that they could no longer even finds words to pray. Then the student read a prayer that had been written by a Christian centuries ago, which was followed with these words: "When I could no longer pray, I let the Church pray for me." Those words were burned into my brain and perhaps even my soul. I was raised in a tradition that placed all the emphasis on "me and Jesus" as the only thing that mattered. Yet, here in this seminary class, I was being invited to see that sometimes we need the people around us to carry us, to say the words we can't find, and to remind us that we belong in all of our complexities. This paralyzed man was fortunate to have such a community around him.

Sometimes we need the people around us to carry us, to say the words we can't find, and to remind us that we belong in all of our complexities.

JESUS HAS A SECRET

Jesus's initial encounter with the man who was blind and his friends seems to have been very public. His entrance into the village was an event that brought people out of their homes and into the streets. So, when asked about healing this man, Jesus's response is interesting: "He took the blind man by the hand and led him out of the village " (Mark 8:23a).

It seems odd, doesn't it? Jesus's response was to take the man by the hand and lead him outside of the village, away from the crowds, and then proceed to heal him. If the point of an act like this is to prove something about Jesus's divinity, why not call the crowd around for this moment? Why not make it a production? Wouldn't it create some word-of-mouth-buzz about the kind of things this Jesus is capable of?

This brings us to one of my favorite, what I like to call, "Bible nerdisms." In the Gospel of Mark scholars have noticed a recurring pattern in which Jesus regularly tries to keep his wonder-working activity off the radar. It's known as the "Messianic Secret," and it comes up again and again throughout Mark's writing. When Jesus performed a sign, or someone recognized him in the role of messiah, he quickly instructed them to keep it to themselves. Some examples might prove helpful.

First, it's an unclean spirit that knows and attempts to identify Jesus:

> Just then there was in their synagogue a man with an unclean spirit, and he cried out, "What have you to do with us, Jesus of Nazareth? Have you come to destroy us? I know who you are, the Holy One of God." But Jesus rebuked him, saying, "Be quiet and come out of him!" And the unclean spirit, convulsing him and crying with a loud voice, came out of him.
>
> (Mark 1:23-26)

And again, later in the same chapter:

> That evening, at sunset, they brought to him all who were sick or possessed by demons. And the whole city was gathered around the door. And he cured many who were sick with various diseases and cast out many demons, and he would not permit the demons to speak, because they knew him.
>
> (Mark 1:32-34)

Then, still in chapter 1, it's a man who had been cleansed of a skin disease:

> After sternly warning him he sent him away at once, saying to him, "See that you say nothing to anyone, but go, show yourself to the priest, and offer for your cleansing what Moses commanded as a testimony to them."
>
> (Mark 1:43-44)

These aren't the only examples, but they serve as examples of what we find over and over throughout Mark's Gospel. I'll share one final passage because it will come up later in the chapter.

Immediately after our story Jesus takes his closest disciples on a little field trip to a place called Caesarea Philippi, a place that would have been scandalous to Jewish visitors. In the name itself we have an homage to both a Roman Caesar (Augustus) and a son of Herod the Great (Philip). In this place Jesus asks his disciples about his own identity:

> Jesus went on with his disciples to the villages of Caesarea Philippi, and on the way he asked his disciples, "Who do people say that I am?" And they answered him, "John the Baptist; and others, Elijah; and still others, one of the prophets." He asked them, "But who do you say that I am?" Peter answered him, "You are the Messiah." And he sternly ordered them not to tell anyone about him.
>
> (Mark 8:27-30)

Why would this be the case? There has been extensive debate and discussion among scholars about this question, and there isn't consensus even today. The most likely scenario in my mind is that Jesus understands the significance of such a claim being made about him, and where it would lead.

Messiah, which means "anointed one" in Hebrew (the Greek is *Christ*), began as a term used for the Jewish kings. They were anointed, literally, with oil at their coronation. The Psalms that celebrate the coronation of the kings even use the language that the descendant of David who sat on the throne was God's son (Psalm 2). Originally, the word *messiah* would have been used to signify anyone who was acting as God's agent in the world. It wasn't a person; it applied to various people over time (even Cyrus, the Persian emperor, in Isaiah 45:1). Eventually, however, the longing for liberation after experiencing the oppression of one empire after another led to a hope that a person would someday arrive on the scene who would take up this role as the Messiah, the one who would send the Romans packing and lead the people to establish liberation, justice, and peace on earth.

This means that then, and now, *messiah* isn't a specifically religious term, but also a political one. To be messiah is to be the rightful king of Israel, which is a claim that will be made about Jesus, by Mark, later in the text. Why would Jesus want to avoid large crowds proclaiming him as messiah? Because that would bring the wrong kind of attention from the occupying Roman forces who recognized no king but Caesar.

This means that Jesus's signs and powerful deeds weren't primarily understood to be just about a physical transformation taking place. These signs were pointing, as signs do, to something larger and far more controversial (and eventually, deadly for Jesus). Jesus's actions of healing, liberating, and even feeding the masses are all messianic challenges to the domination of Rome.

For example, in Mark 5 Jesus encounters a man who was possessed by an unclean spirit. The spirit identifies itself as "Legion," which Mark's readers would understand to be a Roman military term that referred to a unit of six thousand soldiers. Further, when Jesus expelled the unclean spirit, he sends them into a herd of swine, who rush into the sea and drown. This event is so shocking that the locals encourage Jesus to leave their vicinity and to do so as soon as possible.

This story is full of the imagery of the Roman Empire—legions, unclean spirits, swine. These are all symbols of Roman occupation and oppression. Jesus's acts of liberating the man who was possessed and expelling the unclean spirits into the swine who rush into the water are messianic in that they claim that Jesus has the power to bring freedom from Roman oppression. No wonder the people of that village ask him to leave. This is tantamount to treason! As this story concludes Jesus once again encourages secrecy.

As he was getting into the boat, the man who had been possessed by demons begged him that he might be with him. But Jesus refused and said to him, "Go home to your own people, and tell them how much the Lord has done for you and what mercy he has shown you." And he went away and began to proclaim in the Decapolis how much Jesus had done for him, and everyone was amazed.

(Mark 5:18-20)

Jesus encouraged the newly freed man to go home and give the credit to the Lord. Instead, he went off and told everyone about Jesus. Truth be told, the "Messianic Secret" wasn't kept under wraps very well.

WHEN THE MIRACLE DOESN'T TAKE

When the coast was clear, Jesus got down to business.

After spitting on his eyes and laying his hands on the man, he asked him, "Do you see anything?"

The man looked up and said, "I see people. They look like trees, only they are walking around."

(Mark 8:23b-24, CEB)

This story takes a turn when Jesus actually spits on the eyes of the man who was blind. While spitting on someone can be an expression of disgust and dehumanization, spit was also held to have some healing properties and features in many ancient healing stories. While out of place and strange to us, Mark's early audience would've been tracking with the story. There is also another possibility, connected to the Roman emperor Vespasian. According to two Roman historians, Suetonius and Tacitus, the emperor Vespasian was said to have healed a man who was blind by spitting upon his eyes. Is it possible that Mark, writing around the year 70 CE, the same time Vespasian ascended to the Roman throne, is making a bold statement about who Jesus is (and who Vespasian isn't)? At the very least it is interesting to consider.

What happens next is perhaps even more surprising. After Jesus spit and laid hands on the man's eyes, he still couldn't fully see. His sight was only partially restored. He could tell people were around, but the features of those people remained murky. It's evident that both Matthew and Luke made use of the material in Mark when they wrote their own Gospel stories, both making subtle changes at times to the stories they imported from Mark's text. Interestingly, neither Matthew nor Luke included this particular story in their texts. Is it possible they didn't like the optics of Jesus being unable to heal this man on the first try? Undaunted, Jesus takes a second crack at it.

> Then Jesus laid his hands on his eyes again, and he looked intently, and his sight was restored, and he saw everything clearly. Then he sent him away to his home, saying, "Do not even go into the village."

> (Mark 8:25-26)

The second time was the charm. Jesus's touch restored his sight, and what was murky and unclear became sharp and focused. Once again, we have the "Messianic Secret" in full effect, as Jesus sends the man home but with the caveat that he should bypass the village from which they came (and from where everyone saw them leave together). What do we do with such a strange story? Does this story make a statement about Jesus's ability to heal in certain contexts? Or is there something else going on?

WIDENING THE SCOPE

Hopefully something that we've learned over the course of this book is that a story is never really just about that single, isolated event. The writers of the Bible, and this is especially true of the Gospels, aren't trying to just tell one-off stories that are disconnected from the ones that come before and after them. These stories are interconnected and working together to craft a larger narrative. So, with that being the case, let's explore what comes before the restoring of sight to the man who was blind and then what comes after.

The writers of the Bible, and this is especially true of the Gospels, aren't trying to just tell one-off stories that are disconnected from the ones that come before and after them. These stories are interconnected and working together to craft a larger narrative.

Let's rewind to a familiar event in chapter 6. Jesus has drawn a crowd in the middle of nowhere, and his disciples are concerned about how all these people will eat dinner. They want Jesus to disperse the masses to the nearest villages to find food. Jesus would not hear of it.

[Jesus] answered them, "You give them something to eat" (Mark 6:37).

Flabbergasted, the disciples wondered how they could accomplish such a feat. The price tag would exceed eight months' wages! Jesus's solution was for them to bring what they had available—five loaves of bread and two fish—and to organize the crowd of more than five thousand people into groups. Everyone ended up with a full belly, and they collected twelve baskets of leftovers. (I can't help but wonder if they forgot them when they left, as my family often does at a restaurant.) After some extended prayer time alone, this episode is followed by Jesus walking on water to meet his disciples on the lake. Taken together, this feeding and water sign recall the events of the Exodus story, the crossing of the sea and the wilderness feedings.

In chapter 7 there's a controversy about purity issues, and then Jesus healed the daughter of a Gentile woman. That interaction was tense, as Jesus initially refused to help the woman because she was a Gentile (not Jewish). He used an unfortunate image, likening the woman to a dog. Yet, she didn't stop there. She responded in such a way that it stopped Jesus in his tracks. He not only healed her daughter, but others as well, culminating in another mass feeding. This time there were four thousand fed with seven loaves and seven baskets of leftovers.

Following the feeding of the four thousand, and just before our story in which a blind man is healed, Jesus asked his disciples about the mass feedings and the baskets of leftovers.

> Now the disciples had forgotten to bring any bread, and they had only one loaf with them in the boat. And he cautioned them, saying, "Watch out—beware of the yeast of the Pharisees and the yeast of Herod." They said to one another, "It is because we have no bread." And becoming aware of it, Jesus said to them, "Why are you talking about having no bread? Do you still not perceive or understand? Are your hearts hardened? Do you have eyes and fail to see? Do you have ears and fail to hear? And do you not remember? When I broke the five loaves for the five thousand, how many baskets full of broken pieces did you collect?" They said to him, "Twelve." "And the seven for the four thousand, how many baskets full of broken pieces did you collect?" And they said to him, "Seven." Then he said to them, "Do you not yet understand?"

> (Mark 8:14-21)

No doubt those numbers are highly symbolic. The twelve baskets of leftovers after the five thousand were fed call to mind the twelve tribes of Israel. Whatever Jesus is doing, it's about Israel being sustained. Then the seven basketfuls after the feeding of four thousand Gentiles calls our attention to the seven Canaanite nations that the Israelites were called to exterminate from the land during the period of conquest (Deuteronomy 7). Whatever Jesus is doing, it's not about conquest and exterminating the enemy. Instead, Jesus—the new Joshua—and his followers will feed, care for, and include their Gentile neighbors. (I imagine this is why Matthew changes the woman that Mark calls a "Syrophoenician" in Mark 7 to a "Canaanite" in Matthew 15, so it's clear what the connection is.)

That's what comes immediately before our story, but Mark is just beginning to set the table. Following the restoration of sight to the blind man, Jesus has the climactic conversation with his disciples, mentioned before, at Caesarea Philippi. It's there, you'll recall, that Peter recognized Jesus as the Christ, the Messiah, and Jesus responded by once again ordering his disciples to tell no one. Then the conversation took on a heaviness as Jesus began to warn those closest to him about where this journey would lead.

> Then he began to teach them that the Son of Man must undergo great suffering and be rejected by the elders, the chief priests, and the scribes and be killed and after three days rise again. He said all this quite openly. And Peter took him aside and began to rebuke him. But turning and looking at his disciples, he rebuked Peter and said, "Get behind me, Satan! For you are setting your mind not on divine things but on human things."
>
> (Mark 8:31-33)

Imagine the whiplash that Peter and the other disciples must have felt as Jesus shared this ominous warning about the path that was before him. The Messiah couldn't experience defeat; the Messiah would be the great liberator who would usher in an era of justice and peace. For Peter especially, Jesus has gone too far. That's not how a messiah should talk, and Peter begins to call Jesus down for even entertaining the idea that he would die at the hands of Rome.

Jesus matched Peter's energy, calling him Satan in the process. Our assumptions about this word need to be addressed. Jesus is not saying Peter is possessed by a being called Satan. In Hebrew *the Satan* literally means, "the accuser." In the Gospel of Mark, the Satan represents the voice that tempted Jesus in the wilderness to abandon his work as a nonviolent messiah and to, instead, take the shortcut of violence to achieve his goals (Mark 1:12-13, see also Matthew 4:1-11). Peter was now the source of the voice of temptation, and Jesus shut it down quickly.

In the following chapter (Mark 9), Peter once again fails to understand what is happening when Jesus is suddenly and marvelously transfigured before his eyes. Moses and Elijah appear, representing the Law and Prophets, and the light of God rests upon Jesus. In Mark's world, with the Jewish Temple no longer standing, it is likely readers would see this as symbolic of Jesus being interpreted as the new temple. This doesn't mean that Mark is participating in a new religion called Christianity. It means that among the Jewish followers of Jesus, they were trying to make sense of how everything that they had known could be destroyed, and what Jesus meant in the aftermath of an "end of the world" moment for them.

The final episode that will help us understand the two-staged sign Jesus performs in Mark 8 is another miracle event. In this story, Jesus came down from the mountain of transfiguration and found his disciples embroiled in controversy with a large crowd.

A father had brought his son to be liberated from an unclean spirit that had caused his son to be unable to speak. Even worse, the spirit had caused the young man great physical pain and danger as well. The commotion was generated because Jesus's disciples could not free the young man of the spirit. Jesus had to intervene.

> When the spirit saw him, immediately it convulsed the boy, and he fell on the ground and rolled about, foaming at the mouth. Jesus asked the father, "How long has this been happening to him?" And he said, "From childhood. It has often cast him into the fire and into the water, to destroy him; but if you are able to do anything, help us! Have compassion on us!"
>
> (Mark 9:20b-22)

As a parent, I can't help but climb into this father's shoes. That feeling of helplessness when your child needs help beyond what you can muster on your own is terrifying. When our oldest child was around two years old, he had a febrile seizure in the lobby of the urgent care center we had taken him to. His fever went up at such a fast rate that it caused his body to seize up. We had no idea what was happening, but as I held him, yelling for help, I felt absolutely helpless. Thankfully, he was given quick and effective treatment and recovered well. When I think about this father, I'm transported back into that moment in the lobby of the urgent care center. Like us, this father came to the right place.

> Jesus said to him, "'If you can do anything'? All things are possible for the one who has faith."
>
> At that the boy's father cried out, "I have faith; help my lack of faith!"
>
> (Mark 9:23-24, CEB)

Following this exchange Jesus healed the young man, which is where we usually place our focus. For me, however, I always find myself being drawn to this exchange between Jesus and this desperate parent. Jesus's statement about "all things" being possible for the person with faith seems really out of reach for me most days. That seems like a lot of faith, and to be honest, sometimes I can't get all the way there. I have doubts. I have questions. Is there a place for me in Jesus's understanding of faith? The good news for me (and you) is yes, there is room. This father responds with the most honest assessment of our reality: We have faith, and sometimes that faith struggles. At least we want to have faith. It's hard some days, isn't it? Is it possible that the longing for faith is what having faith is all about? Whatever amount of faith this father had, perhaps a mustard-seed-sized amount, it was enough for Jesus. I think it still is.

We have faith, and sometimes that faith struggles.

SEEING THE FULL PICTURE

So, what do we do with this strange story of Jesus restoring the sight of a man who was blind in two stages, and what do all these other stories have to do with it? What if Mark is using this story arc to describe the journey of Jesus's disciples toward understanding who he was and what his work was really about. They had the kind of faith that led them to leave everything to follow Jesus, and yet, they didn't always get what he was saying or doing. It took time for them to grasp the full picture of Jesus's vision of the kingdom of God. The stories before and after the restoration of sight to the man reflect that process and experience of Jesus's disciples in those days between his crucifixion and the Easter experience. Can you imagine how they must have felt? The Jesus they had known, loved, and entrusted themselves to had been brutally executed. Their Messiah was a failure, their hopes dashed. Yet, it was the Easter experience of Jesus as having been raised up by God that helped them see, really see, what Jesus's work and message about the kingdom of God were all about. It was a process for them, and I can't imagine it being any different for us.

THIS STORY TODAY

Let's end with a few takeaways from this story for us today. First, I can't help but be reminded of my experiences in the optometrist's chair, as he flips from lens to lens, asking which is most clear. That's what Jesus was doing with his disciples then, and what he's still doing with us now. The truth is we are always in process. Always. To be alive and human is to be in a continual state of learning to see. If you feel like you don't have it all figured out, or that you still have so much to learn, rest assured that you aren't alone. It should actually give us pause when some think they've already arrived, that they have mastered the Bible or the faith. In this tradition we are all learners, there are no experts.

Second, one of the reasons Jesus's disciples struggled to really see and understand what he was up to is that everything they had learned prepared them for something different. The idea of "failed discipleship" comes up a lot in scholarly discussions of Mark's Gospel. In episode after episode, those closest to Jesus fail to really understand what he's saying and what he's doing. This is most evident on the night Jesus was arrested. His disciples kept nodding off while Jesus was wrestling with his impending suffering. Then, when he was finally taken into custody by Rome, Mark records these painful words: "All of them deserted him and fled" (Mark 14:50).

This statement has the ring of history to it. Why else would Mark choose to include a piece of information that would make the leadership of the early Jesus communities look so cowardly and inept? It was likely common, and deeply regretted, knowledge that, when all the chips were down, Jesus was abandoned by those closest to him.

It's easy to pile on here, as countless sermons have, and look judgmentally upon Peter, James, John, and the rest. "I would have remained faithful," we might protest. Yet, we do have the benefit of hindsight. We experience Good Friday with the information that Easter Sunday is coming. Jesus's disciples didn't. They were trying to make sense of and process traumatic experiences in real time, and their entire lives had taught them to expect something vastly different. Messiahs, real ones, don't get crucified. Yet, they knew they had experienced something real in Jesus, something transformative that had begun to change the way they saw everything.

What if the journey is actually the point? What if there is no other way forward than the sometimes-clumsy path of learning and growing over time? As I write these words, I am a couple weeks away from my forty-first birthday. Over the last four decades I have been multiple people, and each past version of me hasn't disappeared once I left that stage behind. Like the rings of a tree, every version of me has been included in the person I am today. The toddler learning to walk, the five-year-old scared to start kindergarten, the eighteen-year-old with a bad haircut, the self-righteous twenty-year-old preacher boy…you get the picture…they are all still inside me. They no longer drive the bus, but I wouldn't be who I am now without them. That's true for all of Jesus's disciples, then and now, including you. Perhaps, if we can see some of ourselves in them, we might be less judgmental and more compassionate when we read all the ways those who walked with Jesus missed the point. This story, the opening of a person's eyes in stages, is the human experience. It is the way the journey works. It takes time. A lot of patience. Kindness toward ourselves and one another. Transformation is less a microwave and more of a slow cooker.

Because of the COVID-19 pandemic, my oldest missed his annual eye exam in 2020. He's worn glasses since he was small, and most years his vision remains steady, with only slight tweaks to his prescription. He wasn't aware that he wasn't seeing sharply or as focused as he should be because his lenses hadn't been updated for almost two years. When he finally put on his new glasses, he called me and said, "Oh, this is what it's supposed to look like." New lenses made all the difference.

We are all in that process, and I think Jesus has such care and patience for us. There's so much to learn. There will no doubt be moments of misunderstanding and failure along the way. The good news is this: Jesus meets us, not angry, but ready once again to touch our eyes, to update our lenses once again.

"I believe, help my unbelief" is enough, thankfully.

Postscript:
Where Do We Go
from Here?

THE PAST TO THE PRESENT

When I was eleven years old, I was baptized. As a gift my parents gave me a King James Version "Gift and Award Bible." It was black, bonded leather, with gilded edges, and my name and the date of my baptism were embossed on the cover. I had been around the Bible since birth. I knew the gist of most of the major stories and had memorized verses to win prizes in Sunday school. Yet, there was something about getting that Bible that changed things for me. I started to read it. Actually, I devoured it. No one was flannelgraphing (it's a verb) this for me anymore. It was just me and the text, and for the first time I started having questions. I began noticing things that were confusing, things that had been smoothed over and ignored in my memory of how these stories were first told to me. For the first time I was really becoming aware of my childhood lens, and I think now that it was the beginning of my journey toward embracing a grown-up lens. I didn't do that overnight, to be sure. It took time, experience, and education to begin to really see that my questions and curiosities were actually valid and meaningful. But, looking back, it was in an upstairs bedroom in our family home on Pinsonfork Road in McAndrews, Kentucky, that I really began the journey that led to this book.

The Bible is a collection of ancient stories, poems, and letters. They reflect ancient understandings of science, medicine, astronomy, and most everything else. Yet, these same stories, poems, and letters have found a way to remain significant and relevant over the course of three thousand years. How is that possible?

Perhaps the truth is we aren't all that different from our ancient spiritual ancestors. After all, their questions about what it means to be a human being in the world, how we relate to and experience God, why we suffer, and what it means to live a good life while we're here are the questions we still wrestle with today.

Perhaps the truth is we aren't all that different from our ancient spiritual ancestors. After all, their questions about what it means to be a human being in the world, how we relate to and experience God, why we suffer, and what it means to live a good life while we're here are the questions we still wrestle with today. That's why, as we have explored these six stories in detail, I have intentionally connected them to the challenges and opportunities that are before us in our own world. That becomes possible only when we can first appreciate and interpret the stories of the Bible within the contexts that produced them. By better understanding and respecting the past, we can more creatively and faithfully interpret and apply them in the present.

In 1 Corinthians 10, Paul talks about the experience of the Hebrews in the wilderness. After being liberated from bondage in Egypt, they experienced a forty-year period of wandering before reaching the "Promised Land." During that time the people, including their leaders, struggled with faithfulness to God. Paul uses that story to make a connection to the present for the Corinthian church. He writes, "These things happened to them as an example, and they were written down to instruct us, on whom the ends of the ages have come" (1 Corinthians 10:11).

Notice how Paul brings the past and present together. Understanding what happened to them, then, he says, will be helpful to us, now. This isn't unique to Paul, however. Paul is stepping into a tradition that understood and embraced a creative approach to the interpretation of Scripture that was also practiced by Jesus. When embroiled in a debate about the Sabbath in Matthew 12, Jesus calls upon a story from the life of David to explain his approach.

> At that time Jesus went through the grain fields on the Sabbath; his disciples were hungry, and they began to pluck heads of grain and to eat. When the Pharisees saw it, they said to him, "Look, your disciples are doing what is not lawful to do on the Sabbath." He said to them, "Have you not read what David did when he and his companions were hungry? How he entered the house of God, and they ate the bread of the Presence, which it was not lawful for him or his companions to eat, but only for the priests? Or have you not read in the law that on the Sabbath the priests in the temple break the Sabbath and yet are guiltless? I tell you, something greater than the temple is here. But if you had known what this means, 'I desire mercy and not sacrifice,' you would not have condemned the guiltless. For the Son of Man is lord of the Sabbath."
>
> (Matthew 12:1-8)

117

Jesus understood his work, not as an aberration or swerve to the tradition, but as a response to and an outworking of what had come before. The goal isn't to be frozen in the past, but that by understanding the stories and their contexts to be inspired through these stories, poems, and letters to meet the challenges of our own day.

REVISITING WHERE WE'VE BEEN

Before we move on, it might be helpful to step back and just remember the stories we've covered, and how they have connected us, not only to the past but also to our own context, in meaningful and creative ways. In the story of Noah and the Great Flood we saw how human violence became a deluge that threatened to unmake all of creation. As we engaged Noah's story in its ancient context we found connections to the challenges before us today, with the proliferation of violence we see and experience on a global and personal scale. We also began to imagine what "arks," like empathy and compassion, might be accessible to help us stem the tide.

The story of the *Akedah*, the near sacrifice by Abraham of his son Isaac, called for us to acknowledge the difficulties that have been presented by such a story. At the same time, we saw that within its context, the story isn't a celebration of a demanding deity who wants to take our very best from us, but an invitation to a new vision of God, one that provides instead of demands.

The familiar story of Jonah challenged us to look beyond the fantastic elements, the debate of whether or not a human could live in the belly of a fish for three days, and into the meaning of the message Jonah so desperately did not want to share. Jonah calls us to see the universal and expansive love of God and asks us to decide whether we will work in concert with God to share that love, or if we will work against that vision and seek to exclude all the people we don't like or understand.

When we turned to the New Testament, we began with one of Jesus's parables, about a wealthy landowner and his servants. We saw how the meaning and provocative nature of this story is actually obscured by the assumed and traditional interpretation. Then, after contextually reframing Jesus's challenge, we asked how we might find ourselves in situations that call for us to stand with those who are being bullied and harmed by those in power.

We also learned that the story of Zacchaeus, the chief tax collector, is far more challenging than the children's song that has cemented it into our memory. In this story we find a powerful example of what repentance and repair look like, and we hear the invitation to do the same in our own lives. Our participation with God in bringing the "age to come" to bear on the world is not incidental, but essential.

Finally, we looked at what, on the surface, presents as a strange story of a two-staged healing of a man who was blind. As we read the story in the wider context of Mark's Gospel we saw it as reflective of the slow, and sometimes frustrating, pace of Jesus's disciples' journey. Yet we also saw ourselves in them, and found the invitation to keep moving forward, step by step.

WHERE WE GO FROM HERE

I have to confess, narrowing down all of the fascinating, complicated, uncomfortable, and inspiring stories from the Bible to just six was a significant challenge. I would love to have had the space to talk about David and Goliath, the prodigal son, or any number of stories from the Book of Acts. While I didn't have space for all of the stories I wanted to explore—or that you have questions about—these six treatments can serve as a kind of appetizer to spark your curiosity and give you a sense of what is possible as you continue your journey with the Bible (if you choose to continue).

My goal in these pages has not been to keep the recipe a secret, but to offer a glimpse of how we might get more out of our experience of the Bible. If you feel empowered to ask questions, to set aside long-held assumptions, and to enter into these stories with your imagination and curiosity as trusty companions, then I feel like I've done my job. The good news is that this isn't a pass/fail scenario, and the same Spirit that sustained our spiritual ancestors along their journeys remains with us for ours.

As we bring this book to a close, I am reminded of the words of Jesus from John's Gospel. He's preparing his closest followers for his impending absence, and he does so by promising them his continued presence through the Spirit: "I still have many things to say to you, but you cannot bear them now. When the Spirit of truth comes, he will guide you into all the truth" (John 16:12-13a).

Wherever you find yourself—a lover of the Bible, or conflicted and confused by it—the goal of this study is to empower you to ask questions, engage your curiosity, and reimagine what the stories of the Bible might be saying to us. I'm deeply grateful that you have joined me on this journey.

Grace and peace.

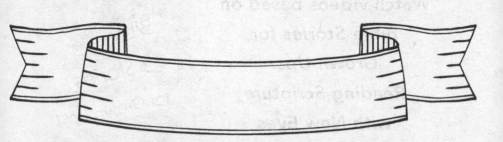

Notes

CHAPTER 1

1. Martin Luther King Jr., "The Casualties of the Vietnam War," speech, The Nation Institute, Los Angeles, CA, February 25, 1967, YouTube video, 38:58, https://www.youtube.com/watch?v=vuySX6Nj1AU.
2. Ashitha Nagesh, "Strangers hold onto man for two hours after he threatens to jump off bridge," Metro UK, May 3, 2017, https://metro.co.uk/2017/05/03/strangers-hold-onto-man-for-two-hours-after-he-threatens-to-jump-off-bridge-6612363/.

CHAPTER 2

1. *Bereishit Rabbah*, *Midrash*, https://www.sefaria.org/Bereishit_Rabbah?tab=contents.
2. From *The Apocrypha and Pseudepigrapha of the Old Testament* by R. H. Charles, Oxford: Clarendon Press, 1913; scanned and edited by Joshua Williams, Northwest Nazarene College, http://www.pseudepigrapha.com/jubilees/index.htm.

CHAPTER 3

1. Rachel Treisman, "A Lobster Diver In Cape Cod Says A Humpback Whale Scooped Him Up And Spat Him Out," NPR, June 12, 2021, https://www.npr.org/2021/06/12/1005918788/humpback-whale-swallowed-lobster-diver-cape-cod-michael-packard#:~:text=A%20Lobster%20Diver%20Was%20Nearly%20Swallowed%20By%20Humpback%20Whale%20Michael,water%2C%20bruised%20but%20otherwise%20unharmed.
2. "Jonah in rabbinic literature," from *The Jewish Encyclopedia*, Isidore Singer, et al., eds. (Funk & Wagnalls, 1901-1906), https://en.wikipedia.org/wiki/Jonah_in_rabbinic_literature.

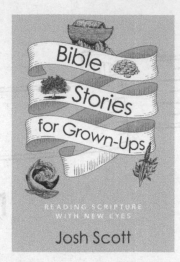